THE END OF THE TABOOS

THE END
OF THE TABOOS

An Ethics of Encounter

GÉRARD FOUREZ

PHILADELPHIA

Fortress Press

Library of Congress Catalog Card Number 72-91522

ISBN 0-8006-0148-3

3232J72   Printed in U.S.A.   1-148

To all those who have
touched my life and whom
I have encountered.

TABLE OF CONTENTS

INTRODUCTION

Today, everything is being questioned. Previously life was more simplified due to the existence of exterior constraints, and a framework of thought which had already been determined by the prevailing agrarian culture. Now, however, because man is assured of the basic necessities of life and is able to allow himself the luxury of leisure, new problems arise. Our society no longer knows what objectives to give to its members and, at the same time, more and more questions are being asked.

In a pre-industrial society, if a young man and woman considered marrying outside their social class, they were faced with a clear-cut choice: they either abided by the customs of society and gave up the idea of marriage or they married and lived on the fringe of society. The concepts underlying these standards are being seriously questioned today, thereby creating more flexible standards of conduct. This contributes to a pervasive instability and notable lack of any definite frame of reference. It is within this context that any study of morality must be pursued today.

Morality (or ethics) is no longer a matter of enunciating norms which are readily accepted; it is rather a case of clarifying the situation in which an individual has to determine his life project. That is why morality is not an objective study of "problems" but the introduction to the mystery of the human. A problem is something you can lay before you and study like a specimen. A mystery is a question that tramples upon and overwhelms its own premises; a question that involves the questioner himself.

The study of morality or ethics is the penetration into the mystery of man. Answers to moral questions will depend on factors such as the degree of commitment at stake and the meaning of the deed expressed. Moral philosophy studies the *meaning* of human conduct, not its *content*; but it is not always easy to distinguish between the meaning and the content of a deed. Two examples may be enlightening.

A child's offering of a bouquet of flowers to his mother is a completely describable act. It can be seen how he gathers the flowers, what he does with them, how he arranges them, etc.; that is, the content of the action is clear. But its meaning may be completely overlooked. We must put ourselves in the place of the mother or the child in order to discover what meaning this gesture has for them. It is only then that the significance of the child's gesture is revealed: he is expressing his love for his mother.

As a second example, let us imagine a couple celebrating their golden wedding anniversary. Suppose they relate to a local newspaper reporter the story of the first time they met. The story as told by the couple may be expressed very differently by the reporter. He is only interested in facts, and anything beyond the scope of the factual presents a problem. For the couple, the event holds a deeper meaning —a meaning which is only fully revealed during fifty years of marriage. For them the meaning is more important than the facts. It is important to realize that the study of the content of an action is not something more "valid" than the study of its meaning. They are simply two different studies. But when the two spouses in the example cited above recount the story of their first encounter, it is much more "real" than the story told by the reporter, because the event itself is so essentially personal.

Moral philosophy studies the meaning of man's actions. But men only exist in particular situations and a valid point of view must take this concreteness of the human condition into account. A philosophical study will thus always be a commitment. It is an activity charged with affective implications, for it engages the whole person—emotion, psyche, and reason. If it were not so this would simply be a sign that the investigation of a philosophical mystery has been reduced to a "problem."

Since the question of life's meaning concerns us all, the investigation of it holds great importance for us and there is a risk that this investigation will be influenced by our own point of view, our fears, our desires, our ideals, and our psychological defenses. Selected questions will be studied simply because of the influence of personal, historical, or cultural factors that have made us more sensitive to these questions than to others. But such a selective choice of study can sometimes be an evasion. There may be a desire to neglect a certain area of reality because one is afraid of it. Since at this level, it is the duty of philosophy to unmask the fraud, the study of morality can be a painful task.

The following pages are reflections on a series of questions arising from human actions. We show that our present moral situation is different from the past and that we are witnessing the end of a morality of taboos—that is, a morality of blind prohibitions. In order to understand the significance of this crisis we must use the resources of several social sciences: sociology, phenomenology, and, of course, psychology. We refer to them in treating such issues as values, fault, and moral conscience. This brings us to distinguish two modes of life; that of the "pioneers" (those who transform their environment) and that of the "nomads" (those who let themselves be transformed by it). The dialectic of the laws of justice and love is then seen as the source of all "good" action.

The second part of the book considers the topic of human development according to Erik Erikson's theory of "the cycles of life." Erikson's life cycles are considered in relation to the development of moral and religious attitudes.

Different avenues of approach to the search for meaning in human actions are presented along with their moral implications. The presentation of such avenues is not at all comprehensive, and still less are the suggestions offered definitive. No solutions will be presented, since beyond the morality of the taboos, it becomes meaningless to tell people what to do. We are only attempting to indicate how certain moral problems can be presented in a new light. We then consider how moral issues are acquiring an increasingly social aspect. It is in this perspective that an ethics of science is envisaged and in such light we propose to view new problems which are now arising to impinge on the realm of moral reflection.

I would like to thank all my friends who have helped me to complete this work. This includes Sister M. Thomas, R.A., the Reverend R. Nugent and Sister Francis Teresa, R.A. for work editing the text and Dr. P. Watte and the Reverend M. Bogaert for contributing their remarks and constructive criticisms.

My special thanks to the staff of Fortress Press and to my friend Ms. June O'Connor without whose editing this book would never have been completed.

My deepest gratitude is due to my students at the Facultés Universitaires N.D. de la Paix, Namur (Belgium), at St. Joseph's College, Philadelphia, Pa., and at the Graduate Department of Religious Education of LaSalle College, Philadelphia, Pa. I have learned from them and they have made this book possible.

I thank also Miss Elizabeth Cavanaugh and Sister Isabel L.S.A. for typing the manuscript.

Finally, I am grateful to all my friends who by their love enabled me to write this book.

Philadelphia
August 1972

PART ONE

THE STRUCTURE OF ETHICS: APPROACHES TO THE PROBLEM OF THE HUMAN SITUATION

CHAPTER I

THE END OF TABOO MORALITY

Human behavior has always varied from one generation to another, but in our day traditional concepts are being challenged more radically than ever. We are in the midst of a crisis of morality.

Everything is being challenged; everything is up for debate. Patterns of living that have kept society stable in the past now appear to be increasingly unstable. For example, the family considered as a sociological entity has changed radically in a very short time. Within one century we have passed from the patriarchal clan to the nuclear family. And now, this nuclear family itself is threatened by the increasing divorce rate. Other institutions that were stable points of reference, such as churches and religious communities, also seem to be on the verge of dissolution. In brief, the patterns of culture which have long been the bulwarks of Western civilization now seem incapable of fulfilling their traditional functions.

Codes of morality are also changing. Forms of behavior which a century ago were absolutely unthinkable are common and are publicly accepted today. Contraception is matter-of-fact; abortion is becoming legalized to an increasing extent; pre-marital sex seems less and less shocking; protests against established authorities, and even revolution have become real possibilities. And yet, in the midst of all this, we are witnessing a new sensitivity in certain areas of morality:

3

an increasing concern for others, a refusal to tolerate social injustice and non-involvement.

In the realm of ideas there has also been a change. On both sides of the Iron Curtain, people are no longer willing to commit themselves to ideologies. One has the impression that, at least at the sociological level, doctrines have lost their impact. "Those who know" or "those who are supposed to know" have become more and more guarded in their statements. And, if they have not been careful to do so, they are considered rather dogmatic and narrow-minded. Science itself is tottering on the pedestal on which it was recently placed. Society has now begun to question science and technology; it has not made man happier; perhaps it is even the cause of the narrowing of man's horizons by enclosing him in a one-dimensional world.

All these changes in attitude show us that a certain number of technical and sociological developments have modified our perception of the world. We are now led to express our ethical values in a new way. Technical and economic progress has liberated man from the demands which once dominated his life, but he now finds himself engaged in more profound thought about ethical values.

The relationship of modern man to his environment differs from that in previous centuries. In former times, people lived a marginal existence. Except for a small group of the privileged, no one was sure of food for the next day. Security became an essential value. Living under the permanent threat of disaster, our ancestors made rules to ensure the status quo. Endangering the stable and established order was inevitably a crime against oneself, one's neighbors, and all of society. Actions, which at first sight seemed innocent, could, because of their social context, become the object of radical condemnation.

In a society which was subject to such economic constraints, norms tended to protect security and stability, even at the cost of suppressing initiative. The social structure had the function of protecting the economic stability of society. This system of protection was generally based on one fact: the interchangeability of roles within the society. Since in a pre-industrial society only limited training was required to assume any role, there were always too many people for one job. The assignment of roles, therefore, was handled by imposing supplementary social and ethical constraints on the members of the group and a rigid status system was developed. The society then structured itself according to social strata rather than according to the differentiation of functions.

In such a society, a person received or was refused a certain role for reasons which were much more related to the conditions of his birth than to the functions required by the role. Probably, the most striking example of this phenomenon is the institution of hereditary royalty and nobility. Although at first sight this system does not seem very efficient (since one can not be sure of getting the "right man"), it does have the advantage of protecting the stability of the society.

Because such stability was important, firm social restraints and repression of all deviations were quite naturally established. Without them, untimely initiatives on the part of individuals would quickly destroy the sometimes hard-won equilibrium of the society. It was therefore imperative that each man would subordinate his own development to the demands of the greatest common good. One had, then, to interiorize the precepts of the society, while at the same time forming goals for one's own life.

At the psychological level, the interiorization of the demands of society upon the individual is the cause of the formation of the superego. According to the manner in which he interiorizes the norms of the group, the individual is made to feel more or less guilty if he departs from those norms. Psychological inhibitions result which (although dependent on the personal history of the individual) are a function of the structure of a given society and civilization.

The constraints we have described explain to a certain extent the characteristics of the ethics we have inherited. It is sometimes called (especially by the disciples of Herbert Marcuse) "repressive ethics." By this is meant that society represses the deviations of individuals in order to build and protect an always threatened civilization. For a better understanding of this process it will be helpful to consider the Freudian concept of civilization.

If we simplify considerably, we can say that, for Freud, man is mainly motivated by his drives which he is never able to satisfy. By nature, man is ever seeking to determine and to possess the object of his desires. At this level he is guided by the "pleasure principle"; but, if he stops there, he will ultimately destroy himself. For survival, man must acknowledge that his life is also determined by the *reality* of his environment. If he does not admit this, not only is he liable to perish, but his life will become sub–human.

In order to humanize his existence, man must repress his desires and channel the liberated energy into the building of a culture and a civilization. He does this by work, apprenticeship, and study. Each of these processes is characterized by the renunciation of an immediate satisfaction for the sake of changing the environment. Man thus represses his natural drives in order to develop a culture; only then does his relationship to the world and other men become human and civilized. His repressed drives are sublimated into meaningful goals and meaningful relationships.

For Freud, the adoption of a moral law (always more or less repressive) by a society is the expression of this need to repress man's basic drives. The moral law is the statement of the necessary repression of natural satisfaction for the sake of human development. Contrary to a common stereotype, Freud does not offer a lax morality but rather the opposite. For him the energy from which civilization can be built is provided by the repressed libido. In the same way, sexual desire which a person renounces can be invested in the brotherly love of friendship. What Freud protests against is an *unhealthy* repression of the libido.

Our traditional ethical system may thus be seen as a protection for civilization and its values: work, instruction, and performance. This is the repressive aspect of morality. In other words, tradition has bequeathed to us a morality of commandment. Commandments excuse one from the necessity of too much reflection; good as well as evil is defined by law. The code protects the established order of things. In obliging man to repress excessive spontaneity it draws upon the basic mechanism of repression essential to human psychology.

Constructed upon such assumptions, a morality of commandment almost necessarily tends to be heartless. The protection of the social order imposes the duty of punishing every deviation. We have only to remember how society has dealt with unwed mothers, homosexuals, and those who have entered into interracial marriages. Actually the insistence on values connected with marriage and sexuality is connected with the desire for stable lines of succession. Since it aims for the survival of civilization, such a morality is necessarily "investment" oriented. A child is wanted not only for his value as a person but for what he will bring to the family. It is indeed almost impossible not to see in our traditional morality, elements of a morality of investment and profit.

Seen in such a perspective, moral life is protected and strengthened by means of pressure and control. The individual who does not conform to the demands of the group takes the risk of being isolated or excommunicated.

As a supplementary means of control, traditional morality

7

appeals to the authority of the "sacred." Just as pre-industrial society was structured along the lines of social status rather than of personal function, so its values were, to a great extent, honored because they were of long-standing and not because they were inherently meaningful. Morals then were not important for what they were in themselves but because they had been "sanctified" by a more-or-less divine authority. At the extreme, the reasons for the existence of a certain moral prescription were completely forgotten and the prescription had value *only* because it was "given by the gods." For example, divorce was considered "wrong" because it was an "offense against God" or a disruption of the social order. The fact that it was a failure of the love between two persons was not considered to be relevant.

The traditional morality of our society, whose principal goal is its own self-preservation, has led to a "performance mentality." The importance of performance has so entered into our ethical concepts that most people today feel "guilty" the minute they stop producing. Such things as simply enjoying life, being in the company of a friend, taking time to reflect, to be truly present to others, doing something just for the fun of it, accepting the love and appreciation of others—none of these is completely "acceptable" within the framework of traditional morality. Spontaneity must give way to the "serious things" of life! In this frame of reference the importance of repression and inhibition in the task of building a culture is underlined and the demands of morality appear primarily as limitations to the person.

This is a correct interpretation of traditional morality but it is nonetheless incomplete. We must also consider the positive outcomes of man's repression of his spontaneity. To cite only one example: the repression of the sex drive for the sake of the institution of marriage is the means of developing a real love or friendship within marriage—a love that is both sexually fulfilling and human in the highest sense. As was mentioned above, the repression of a desire is accomplished and accompanied by the choice of a human "ideal." One can look at ethical prescriptions from this viewpoint and see their positive aspects. Ethics then appears as the building of a meaningful and personal life. One of the problems of morality today is precisely the balance of these two aspects: (1) To what extent is it good to suppress spontaneity? and (2) How can we reconcile the demands of building a civilization with the desire to be loved and valued and personally fulfilled as individuals?

A second comment concerns the criticism that we have exaggerated the repressive aspect of moral codes. Morality, as will be noted, has always promoted man's total fulfillment; it has taught him how to achieve a meaningful and authentic existence. These observations are quite correct, but they are merely emphasizing the positive aspects of moral obligation. This emphasis runs the risk of confusing the ideal and the real, what is theorized or taught, and what is lived behaviorally.

It is indeed important to realize that in questions of morality (as in many other areas) one cannot only idealize. Sociological research has shown that there is a vast gap between the ideal morality created by intellectuals and the real value systems by which most people live. Intellectualized morality can provide guidance and motivation for action, but it would be naïve to believe that real motivations are as easy as those described in books.

In present Western civilization, economic constraints have relaxed considerably. For the greater part of the population, the threat of hunger has vanished; there are no longer so many reasons to fear existence. At the same time, social structures are evolving rapidly. Assignment of roles is not based on "natural" differences of status but rather on individual competence. These roles are becoming increasingly diversified and call for specialization. Personal initiative is no longer feared, but, on the contrary, considered as one of the main instigators of progress. Society as a whole has become more tolerant. Differences of opinion no longer threaten a breakdown of relations, and openness to people of different ideologies and behavior is now accepted. In a word, the various pressures exerted by environment, economy, society, and ideologies have greatly decreased. Modern man thus finds himself more liberated; he can reflect upon his emancipation from the tutelage of a repressive morality. This change in morality has been developed by Herbert Marcuse.

Marcuse distinguishes between a "performance principle" and a "reality principle." According to the reality principle, man is willing to delay present pleasure for the sake of building the human relationships which give meaning to his life. On the sociological plane, this gives rise to culture. But, Marcuse states, this repression of spontaneity is liable to become an end in itself and, in time, man will no longer act according to the reality principle but according to the performance principle.

The supreme value then becomes the suppression of spontaneity for the sake of . . . one does not know what. Man no longer accepts limitations in order to adapt himself to reality, but just because "it has always been done." It was necessary to repress spontaneity in the past, so he continues to do so now. His activity, instead of being a liberating factor, becomes the means of sustaining a civilization in which life resembles that of a forced–labor camp.

What is worse, this production is not demanded by a man with whom one could have a personal relationship (even if it were that of "exploited" and "exploiter"), but by an impersonal organization. The organization, the social and economic system—and sometimes morality itself—by their very impersonalization achieve a kind of existence in themselves. They become for man the prisons in which he himself is the keeper. As long as he follows the performance principle man forgets that he has a right sometimes just to "be himself." Finally, he no longer knows how to play, to be poetic, to be artistic—to enjoy life.

The fault of this system lies in the fact that in a world where man has become liberated from many natural pressures, the system still fosters the attitudes needed when constraint was necessary for culture. When he realizes what is happening, man rebels and spontaneity claims its rights. It is here, perhaps, that we will find the source of the present moral crisis.

We are witnessing a kind of rebellion of the spontaneous man against a society based on the performance principle. There is opposition to all control, whether it comes from morality or some social organization. This accounts for the utopian attitudes of certain hippie communities. Even if these groups are not very constructive, they can be quite instructive. They confront society with the reality of the rejection of all law, with concern for suffering, with the refusal to worry about the future because they want to fulfill themselves "now," with the watering down of differences between groups, with the rejection of all taboos from whatever source, with the enhancing of sincerity, spontaneity, from sexual expression, and personal fulfillment. All this can be summed up in their own slogan "Make love, not war." In short, they manifest to the contemporary world the rebellion of spontaneity against oppression. But where will all this lead? Will the present revolt against moral repression—if it ever is successful—initiate an era of spontaneous and innocent freedom or will it lead to chaos, barbarism, and the destruction of all civilization?

Authors differ on this question. Marcuse and Freud, for example, have diametrically opposing views on this subject.

Marcuse thinks that the abandonment of the production principle will open up new horizons for man beyond which there will no longer be such things as aggressiveness, dependence, and alienation. Work would still be part of such a society but it would be humanized, spontaneous, and enjoyable. Sexuality itself would be transformed. It would no longer be limited to genitality and reproduction but it would become the normal expression of an affectionate encounter with another.

Freud, on the contrary, was convinced that if the present repressive system should collapse, it would mean catastrophe. If man's drives are liberated, we will return to barbarism, inhuman struggle, and finally the end of all culture.

So, we see civilization's great dilemma: Should the repression of spontaneous personal development continue or must we face the risk of chaos in liberating life? It is in this question that the present crisis in the development of moral theory is situated. If the new schools of thought choose the road of repression they will probably be rejected by future generations; but if human desire is not channeled, where will it lead?

In order to reconcile these apparently opposite poles perhaps we should now consider a personalized reality principle which would not suppress spontaneity. This principle would take into account the two activities which (according to Freud) must be reconciled if human balance is to result; these two activities are love and work.

The theories of Freud and Marcuse have both advantages and disadvantages. Marcuse reinstates human spontaneity to its proper place; he denounces the useless tyranny of "inhuman organizations" and proposes a liberation which can only be good. The problem is that one cannot really see where it all leads. Moreover the "spontaneous man" of Marcuse, in the long run, stands alone. He enjoys life without guilt and in harmony with nature; he is spontaneous and self–centered. But is he really human? Is he really capable of personal encounter? On the other hand, Freud very keenly demonstrates the need for channeling human spontaneity, but one wonders why and for whom? Insofar as the reality principle is impersonal, Freudian repression is a heavy burden to bear. Is there another alternative?

What could break the dilemma is a reality principle which would be lived in a personalized fashion. In this perspective, morality would not be seen as an abstract commandment (whether it be a categorical imperative or a divine order), but as the exigency of encounter with another or "The Other." At this point, moral reflection could leave the solipsism of Marcuse and the stoicism of Freud, if we can so caricature them, and set out upon a more personal approach. Morality would be then based on the loving encounter of people. Clearly this point of view is not new, but is the ideal of the Christian gospel whether or not it is in fact lived by most Christians. For Christ, all morality is summed up in the love of God and neighbor, the neighbor being seen as every human being.

Obviously, to develop a morality which would make an absolute of the love and respect due to persons is just as bad as one which makes an absolute of certain precepts. There is a need to explain what is meant by stating that love is the basis of ethics. In answering that question, a system of morality will be constructed which will try to express the demands of justice and love within a particular culture. Any precepts which result will be relative to the culture which produces them; nevertheless they will also express man's need to recognize the presence of another or The Other who is different from himself. It is interesting to note that, in this respect, anthropologists have identified two acts which are somehow prohibited in every culture: incest and murder.

The structure of the experience of encountering the

other merits further description. It is the analysis of this structure which will determine the ethical beliefs of a society, that is, the teaching handed down concerning the meaning of actions.

The essential element in an encounter is not so much the fact that "I meet another" but rather that "another summons me." An encounter is not just something I *do*; rather, I allow it to happen. The other reveals himself to me as different in such a way that I cannot reduce him to the dimensions of my idea of him nor my desire for him. It is to this experience that we referred when we mentioned the possibility of a personalized reality principle. The other is revealed as different, and it is exactly this difference which makes me realize that I, too, am different—I am myself—a unique being with a unique set of responses.

An encounter is thus a two–way experience; I am summoned, unveiled, and touched through the presence of another who makes me realize that I am a person. The other asks me to let myself be loved by him, to let myself be encountered so as to be able to encounter him. For this to be possible, however, he also invites me to renounce certain immediate satisfactions so as truly to meet him. He asks me to respect his identity as a person in his own right. These two elements (the acceptance of myself as someone who is loved and the acceptance of the other as someone who is to be respected) cannot be experienced without producing a certain amount of fear. Indeed, an encounter is the experience of the passage from fear to trust. In the end, one trusts oneself as capable of respecting the other, while trusting the other as capable of truly loving. When life is lived at this level, it is not controlled by constraints and exterior prohibitions. It is a more full response to a call that is addressed to me, individually. This call can be perceived in many different ways. For some it is the call of another who draws me out of my loneliness and who is a human being like I. For others, it is the call of The Other who loved us first when we were not yet worthy of being loved. It must be carefully noted that this call, although it influences people's lives, is never oppressive. The Christian tradition of a liberating God, loving to the extent of serving others, can be quite enlightening here. The freedom of the Christian (together with respect and compassion for others) has, perhaps, not always been taken seriously enough. Fundamentally, Christian ethics should never be marked by fear for "Perfect love casts out fear." (I John 4.18)

The task of the moral philosopher, then, is to study the structure we have just described and to draw values from it which will form an ethic. Acts will no longer be evaluated according to exterior criteria but according to the degree to which they are meaningful. In some sense, it has always been the meaning of an act which has set its value, but, in the wake of the "collapse of constraints," significance has been less rigidly defined. The result of this change of attitude is seen both in the refusal to accept any kind of absolute "Thou shalt not . . ." and in the depth of reflection upon the real meaning of any act.

As an example, let us take the classic case of pre–marital sex. Until now, the situation was clear; even those who did not follow civil law admitted its existence. Today, many young people cannot see any reason why there should be such a law. The development of this change of attitude is interesting to study.

The situation began with a law demanding very little reflection; pre–marital sex was forbidden and that was that. If someone asked for an explanation the answer was easy; even if one did not appeal to "divine law," it was enough to point out the consequences of having a child out of wedlock. There was no possible alternative and, since the act was obviously wrong, there could be no exception to the law. However, today these reasons do not hold. With the

15

advent of wide–spread use of contraceptives, the risk of pre–marital sex is no longer self–evident.

Unless we choose to take refuge behind a "divine law" (which would make God an arbitrary judge who refuses to explain his decisions) we are now forced by reality to rethink in depth the meaning of sex, both in and out of marriage.[1] We move then from an externalized moral law to a morality of meaning which is much less rigidly defined and, therefore, much more flexible. This is not to say that a morality based on meaningfulness will be more lax than a morality based merely on prohibitions; it is merely looking at the situation from a different point of view and, therefore, perhaps, looking more deeply.

The question now is how to ascertain, in a given situation, which path of action will help the participants and others to grow in love. This type of thinking does not eliminate the idea of the "absolute" in morality; it merely re-situates it. The absolute is not to be found in a given norm of behavior or in a social convention; it is only discovered in the mystery of encounter with another or The Other.

Taken from this perspective, the moral law does not disappear. Its function is the elaboration of the theory based on the meaningfulness of acts. The only "commandment" is that we should love and respect the other—whether with a small or capital "o." The value of any act has to be judged on the basis of how it expresses this law of love. In general, when an act expresses a refusal to love, it is considered "immoral." Thus, since murder is not usually an expression of love, the moral law states "Thou shalt not kill."

So we see the law playing a double role. In the first instance it plays the part of teacher and from it each man

---

1 If one understands "divine law" as a decree of God upon man, it is probably appropriate to say that such a law does not exist. Eventually, the God to whom such a law was attributed would only be an idol (cf. the last sentence of the Epistle of John).

learns the significance of his actions. But it is also a challenge because the existence of a developed theory of morality calls a man to transcend himself and to accept the fact that his acts have a significance which goes beyond his own little "island."

In this way the law opens man to the dimensions of worldwide justice. In accepting law man accepts a definition of "justice" toward others. The acceptance of this need for justice expresses respect for the other and prevents the development of a pseudo–love which would be intruding and possessive. In short, the law (seen in this light) is not something *imposed* upon man, but society's expression of the fact that we are always in the presence of someone "other" than ourselves.

The relaxation of economic, social, and psychological constraints in modern society has led to new insights regarding morality. Despite the depth of its ideals the "old" morality[2] was lived out in submission to the principle of performance rather than to the principle of reality. In extreme cases, man repressed his spontaneity entirely and identified himself totally with his task. In face of the still real tendency in this direction shown by our one-dimensional culture, man's spontaneity is beginning to rebel. But rebellion also means risking the possibility of wandering aimlessly through the chaos of human impulse or through the structureless world of the "hippies."

In response to this situation it seems possible to present a morality based upon the encounter with another, The Other. It would reinstate the principle of reality but in a per-

---

2 Let us again insist on the fact that by the term "traditional morality" we do not designate morality as it has genuinely been lived in depth by many but morality as it has often been perceived in our past society as a series of prohibitions. Nobody had to wait for Marcuse to hear a protest against the ethics of the law; the gospel and Christian thought are filled with protest against the repressive ethics of the Pharisees.

17

sonalized manner. The difference between this emerging morality and morality as it was often lived in the past is found in the part played by the law. In traditional morality there was a tendency to make the law an end in itself. There could be no further moral reflection and in some instances it became a morality of taboos.

In the new vision of the moral order the law is seen as mediating the development of man; like a teacher, it opens up broader horizons and extends man's view to the dimensions of universal justice. Through this mediation it gives man the opportunity to direct his activity in a meaningful manner. This passage from the law as "end" to the law as "means" is very aptly expressed in the gospel of the Christian scriptures when Jesus said in reference to the sabbath: "The law is made for man, not man for the law." For this point of view, nothing is "taboo" or forbidden; but values are suggested as possible choices. No one can determine solutions to ethical questions. People will simply exist in the way they make themselves be.

For Further Reading

Freud, Sigmund, *Civilization and Its Discontents* Jean Riviere, trans., (New York: Cape and Smith, 1930).

A presentation of Freud's view of civilization's great dilemma: is man forced to choose between repression and chaos?

Marcuse, Herbert, *Eros and Civilization* (Boston: Beacon Press, 1966).

This is Marcuse's study of the tensions at play between the pleasure principle, the reality principle, and the performance principle. The book is more difficult than others in this bibliography but is worthwhile reading.

_____, *One Dimensional Man* (Boston: Beacon Press, 1964).

A study of alienation in contemporary society, dominated as it is by the performance principle.

CHAPTER II

THE HUMAN SITUATION: SOCIOLOGICAL— PHENOMENOLOGICAL— PSYCHOLOGICAL

Before we give further consideration to the meaning of human activity, let us look objectively—and with as few a priori assumptions as possible—at how men value.

For the sociologist, a value is something accepted and desired by the members of a society (e.g., cutting off heads among the Jivaros, the democratic ideal among Americans, the norms governing sexual life in every civilization, etc.). Every society builds a system of values; accepting this system simplifies life and makes corporate effort possible without too many difficulties. It is useful to distinguish two kinds of values which we will call "theoretical values" and "real values."

A theoretical value is a type of action which is approved by the people of a particular society. It involves a way of evaluating human activity: "x" is good, "y" is bad. "Right–thinking people" are people who believe in these theoretical values. Theoretical values, then, are intellectual notions; they are what men say is good. Real values, on the contrary, are what men actually do and approve of in practice. Real values stem from actions and not from words.

These two types of values may be very different. For example, in nineteenth century bourgeois society the theoretical value of marital fidelity was strongly defended, but in actual practice the bourgeois man who kept a mistress met with little disapproval from society if he was sufficiently discreet. Today, there exists in the West a highly esteemed theoretical value which says that rich nations should help poor ones. The real situation, however, shows that such aid is rarely given.

Even if theoretical values are not always accepted in practice, this does not mean that they are irrelevant. They are the conceptual framework by means of which a particular society's theory of human behavior can be elaborated. It is to this theory that a society appeals to face its problems. As the members of a society become aware that there is an increasing distance between their theoretical and real values, they will attempt to bring their actions back into line with their theoretically accepted values. For example, in the United States the ideal model is that of a peaceful and friendly people; actual practice, however, often reveals economic and military imperialism. Lately, many Americans have come to realize the distance between their theoretical values and their real values. In this way theoretical values can be a cause of behavior modification.

A sociologist will take as his task the description of these values. His role is not to give an appreciation of a society's "ideal," but only to identify the elements of this ideal. From this sociological viewpoint let us examine how a system of values is structured.

A type of action is a value if it is considered desirable by a society and is economically or emotionally sanctioned by the members of that society. But no society ever recognizes as acceptable a single isolated value. Each particular value is one element of a composite which is agreed upon to some degree by the entire society. This community of values is obvious when people give the same reasons to explain why they do certain things. If there is insufficient agreement in a society concerning proper and improper conduct, conflicts will arise. It is important that the group work to solve such conflicts for if they cannot do so peacefully, violence may result. A civil war, for example, is a conflict of values which is resolved through violent means.

Reasons vary as to why people esteem certain values. Some values will be esteemed because they permit the society to function smoothly (e.g., good organization). Other values arise from the experiences of social life, qualities which cause a person to be esteemed by other members of the society (e.g., being an attractive or intelligent person). Also there are values which are justified by an ideology or by their relationship with the final end of man (e.g., religious systems). These general concepts normally serve to structure the entire set of values into a single system.

The value system of a given society never remains static, but is always evolving. This process is sometimes carried out through social conflicts. Every society has institutions whose function it is to resolve these value conflicts; these institutions are indispensable for the survival of the group. Courts, for example, are institutions whose function is the solution of conflict; wars are also institutionalized conflicts.

Sociologists have discovered that in practically all civilizations, the ultimate values revolve around the concepts of friendship, love, and justice. This well-known fact merits serious reflection in the attempt to develop an ethical system.

Having looked at how the sociologist views men's values, it is pertinent to consider also the phenomenon of deviations.

For the sociologist, a deviation is a human behavior which is divergent from the values accepted by the society. It has to do with what is considered to be abnormal or non-conformist with respect to the system of values of a particular society. Because society always tries to protect itself against deviants, man has a tendency to seek security within a well–organized whole. Nevertheless, for things to function smoothly, society must accept certain deviations from its ideal. For survival purposes, society may allow certain ideal values to become blurred. This was one of Machiavelli's discoveries: he accepts as necessary for political functioning a certain number of non-values. Without these, he says, it would not be possible to govern.

Some deviations can be considered "positive." These are those which are finally approved by the society. Though divergent from the general norms of a society, the positive deviations do not really exclude what that society regards as its final ends. Consequently, the deviations are ultimately approved, although perhaps only after serious tensions. Such deviations not only gain a certain tolerance by the society, but they even have a very specific role to fulfill. The prophets and saints in a society are the positive deviants who recall to that society its theoretical and final ends.

Even negative deviants can be very useful. For example, in the United States the violence of the Black Power movement makes deviant non-violent movements more acceptable and enables them to make their message heard. Negative deviation, then, is sometimes advantageous and even necessary for progress.

Deviations, whether positive or negative, may become institutionalized. Such is the case, for instance, in espionage, prostitution, political protest groups, and religious communities. A society may also include entire sub-groups which have adopted a different scale of values. These will be labeled "deviant sub-groups." Examples include isolated religious sects such as the Amish, certain political parties as Nudist Party, and homosexual groups such as the Gay Liberation Front.

In this discussion we have studied the way in which sociology views the existence of value systems and deviations, their function in society, and the gap between theoretical value systems and actual behavior. But sociological evidence obviously lacks one essential element, namely, a perception of the meaning of actions from within. To expand our consideration of the moral experience we will analyze how individuals open themselves to the possibility of having committed a fault for which they will assume the final moral responsibility.

A fault can be seen as a "blemish" or "stain," something distasteful or ugly which mars or "dirties" the personality. In this view, a fault is reified, having an existence which is static and for which one is not responsible. An individual so marked is imposed with the duty of purifying himself from it.

Seeing certain norms of action as taboo corresponds to his kind of thinking: if I do this, I will be marked. This is a morality of prohibitions in which man lives under the threat of something which can destroy him and over which he has little control. He can be overcome by it and is liable to be afflicted by destiny. Greek tragedy often describes these situations. Oedipus, for example, will finally be annihilated by the destiny which destroys him. Yet he is not responsible for it; he is not guilty. There is in him something not of his own choosing, but which nonetheless affects him. At this level of awareness, man undersands that he is something which he does not want to be. The Christian outlook incorporates this aspect of fault as a social flaw, an "original sin," defining it as sin "anterior to free will."

Faced with this situation, man wonders what happens and asks why it is so. Upon reflection, the fault appears as a "transgression" against a set of ideals which assumes the image of a command, a law, an obligation. It no longer seems to be simply something passive, but the result of a

25

negative action; human responsibility is now involved. From this responsibility a structure of what "ought to be" emerges and is known as "the moral law." The law is a statement of what one ought to do, the set of values as they "ought to be" held. At the same time it creates the concept and the possibility of judgment.

This discussion has disclosed a shift in the perception of fault from something passive which happens to us, to something actively chosen and engaged in; from something which weighs "on the conscience" to something for which I hold responsibility. Nevertheless, even thought of in this way, a fault, unfortunately, can still be reduced to a "problem," to an object of intellectual reflection, to a "situation" separate from one's own being.

The most honest step is taken when the fault is not only reflected upon by man, but also admitted by him. Man says, "It is I who have sinned; I am standing before others as a sinner; it is as such a limited person that I request acceptance from you." In saying this, he discovers a growing awareness of something new in his life: the experience of sin and the need for forgiving acceptance. Now the fault no longer seems to him like a stain from without or a transgression of a given norm, but as something interior and personalized. He becomes aware, now, that he is the one who has caused the alienation from his very self, from others and from the world. He realizes that he is responsible.

In this experience of facing another, he realizes that he is not living on the level of persons.

Herein lie the beginnings of situating oneself in truth in a world of persons. The individual faces up to others: he accepts being unmasked. Placing himself in a personal universe he opens himself to others and to love and forgiveness. He calls himself, both in his own mind and before others, a sinner. His relationship to others now includes the concept of forgiveness, which is not condescension toward him but radical acceptance of him. For a love which does not ask for forgiveness or which does not know how to forgive is not yet perfect; it is, in fact, a very shallow love.

According to the degree of his awareness of fault, man develops differing views of ethics. At the level of the taboo, he is caught in a situation which he cannot control. His morality, then, is one of terror; the result is a fear that the world will turn against him, that he will always be the prey of destiny. He then tries to save himself by superstitious practices, rituals, or fixed formulae of prayers. He does not live in a personalized world, but in an oppressive universe.

If man achieves an insight into fault as transgression, he still fears the effects of the transgression. But this is no longer terror because he realizes the cause of the fear. It is, nonetheless, fear. He asks, "Will not the world I have wounded, the harmony I have destroyed, also destroy me? How can I set things straight and do what I should have done?" He regards himself as having disrupted the established order.

At a deeper level, when man finally acknowledges himself as sinner, he becomes aware of living in relationship with others and with God. He sees too that he is not "authentic" in his own existence. There may even appear a certain anguish; is forgiveness possible? Is it still possible to love? To this basic question, we suggest (along with Christian tradition) that love consists in mutual forgiveness and acceptance, converting the very obstacles between persons into a bond of union. A love which extends even to forgiveness, which understands that it is as fitting to receive love as it is to give love without thought of self, goes beyond fear and anguish. The moral law becomes an expression of the choice of loving.

This brief sketch of the phenomenology of the experience of the fault can be further augmented by the contributions of modern psychology, especially the insights of Freud.

It is important to remember that Freudian concepts such as the "Oedipus conflict," the "libido," the "death instinct," and similar terms do not refer to historical or material realities. These are expressions that tell us something about the reality of man and to understand them, we must do more than consider their direct literal content. The theory of psychoanalysis resembles a myth, a story which, without claiming to be materially true, tells us something about ourselves.

It must be noted here that in the framework of this study, only a rough sketch of depth psychology can be presented.

According to Freud, man has within himself drives which urge him to go outside himself; these life drives are called "eros" or "libido." Libido can be more or less correlated with "sexuality," if the latter is understood to imply more than simple genitality. At any rate, it is important to be aware that all human behavior is more or less imbued with the reality of man's sexual being. Eros is the vital impulse which forces man beyond himself.

The infant who opens himself to the world and clings to his mother nevertheless discovers quite soon that he cannot possess the whole world and especially not his own mother. In fact, he notices that he must share her affection with his father. The father somehow appears as an obstacle to what he wants. At this point, because he wants to take his place, the infant experiences what psychoanalysts sometimes call the "desire to kill the father." The child must resolve this tension. Since he cannot really enter into competition with someone who seems to have all power and strength, he has to repress his feelings. But then he must come to terms with his opposition to his father in some other manner. The Oedipus conflict can be solved in a variety of ways.

The child can accept the authority of the father, aware of the fact that he cannot compete with him. He then sees in his father a hero whom he admires and loves. There is in this solution of the conflict a sort of idealizing of the father. Later on, when the child has matured, the situation hopefully evolves into a true friendship with the father. Since friendship presupposes equality, this evolution will, in the end, allow a man to find his place among others as a brother among brothers.

If the child does not succeed in discovering a hero in his father he is liable to bear a repressed hate over the years. In this case, he will show an "authority complex" in his adult life. Any authority figure will awaken in him this same more or less repressed hate. Whatever he has not yet accepted in relation to his own father is projected onto all authority and all rule–making. He wants to reject all norms and all constraints.

From this conflict there arises what psychology calls "the law of the father." The "law of the father" is the hold of reality on the child and it is this which he must accept in the Oedipus conflict. Insofar as the conflict is poorly resolved (and it is never completely resolved by anyone) this "law of the father" is submitted to with hate. The remnants of this more or less unresolved conflict always remain as part of man's psychological background and every law awakens in him a feeling of revolt and of oppression. If this conflict is resolved in a healthy manner, this "law of the father" appears as an ideal to be followed and law then becomes both a prohibition and a promise.

This law of the father does not refer only to the Oedipal situation, but has far greater implications, since every law and rule is reacted to in reference to the way in which the law of the father is perceived. It is a component of the moral conscience.

Consequent to the Oedipus conflict, Freud distinguishes three levels in the structure of the personality: the "id," the "superego" and the "ego."

The id is the psychic expression of the drives of the individual, the tendencies and feelings which are in him, making him desire something or act in a certain way. The id is, for Freud, the reservoir of psychic energy. People sometimes refer to it spontaneously in such expressions as "It (id) was stronger than I."

The superego is the internalized law of the father and the group. In the Oedipal period, the child finds a law imposed on him which he is obliged to follow. In order to avoid being dominated by the law and living in permanent conflict, he identifies with it. Thus that level of the personality is formed by which the child interiorizes the law of the father and, later, all other laws which he has to accept. The superego records the behavior which the culture and the society impose on the individual.

This level of psychological structure is very important for it is the source of civilization. It is because man unconsciously accepts the need to repress his desire for natural enjoyment, to delay certain satisfactions, to obey the commandments of society, that it becomes possible for him to make an investment in the world. Learning or working— and every human culture is based on work and learning— demand this kind of investment. Man accepts not enjoying everything at once in order to build for himself a world and a culture that is human. The interiorization of the law of the father which puts off satisfactions until later is, therefore, essential to the building of a civilization. This does not happen without creating problems. The superego is blind internalization, imposed, like the id, in an irrational fashion.

The third level of the personality is that which will arbitrate the conflict between the superego and the id in the face of reality. This is the ego. The ego can be thought of as a steering wheel by which man attempts to adapt himself to reality and to act according to what he thinks best. The adult man shifts onto his ego a good number of commandments which are stamped on his superego; he then begins to act rationally. A man's growth implies that his decisions no longer completely depend on the blind id or superego, but increasingly on his conscious ego. This also corresponds to a transformation of the role of the father. The "absolute-authority-father" becomes the "father-friend." One passes from the realm of terrifying authority to friendship, and at the same time from fear of the law to use of the law.

Under the reign of fear, the law of the superego dictates conduct and threatens him who dares violate an order. But if behavior is decided at the level of the ego, the person accepts the limits imposed by the law because he sees this law as a mediation, as something which allows him to accomplish his goal as a man. The superego corresponds to the unconscious repression[1] of inadmissible actions and feelings; the ego corresponds to the renunciation of certain actions, the conscious suppression of certain feelings and the construction of a personal ideal. Repressive processes, that is both repression and suppression, usually involve sublimation. This latter utilizes the energy which "naturally" would be directed to other ends by unconsciously directing it toward new goals. Thus sublimated sexual energy, according to Freud, builds civilization and becomes culture.

In our actions we sometimes experience a certain malaise. Our conscience reproaches us for something we have done. This feeling is associated with one of the psychological levels we have described above—the superego. Our

1 Repression is the unconscious elimination of feeling. Suppression is the process by which a feeling, which is acknowledged and accepted as real, is eventually excluded from consciousness because the ego decides it is better not to let it develop.

"conscience," which is the monitor of the unconscious, censures our action. The feeling aroused by this censure brings information with it; it points out some contradiction between what we have done and the commands which we have interiorized during our psychological evolution. This feeling, however, does not necessarily bear any relationship to the validity of the information. It may well be that our superego is indeed setting off a kind of alarm because our action was really a refusal to love. (It would then function as a "well-formed conscience.") But it is just as possible that the alarm set off by the superego is not appropriate.

The possibility that the conscience can be "wrong" arises from the fact that this superego structure is not received ready–made but is gradually formed throughout an individual's history. For reasons which are involved with the way the Oedipal conflict was resolved, certain actions are censured by the superego; when we violate its prohibitions, a feeling of guilt arises in us. Mature people do not react blindly to this feeling. A true adult learns to shift this feeling onto the conscious ego, and thus judges the goodness of his act according to the degree to which it expresses what he wants to be. It is important that we investigate the role of guilt feelings and learn how to interpret this psychological "alarm."

Guilt feelings should not be repressed. To repress something is to shut one's ears to a certain part of reality. It usually does no good, for what is repressed continues to affect the person at unconscious levels, and normally reappears in another area, quite often in an unacceptable way. If, however, a feeling of guilt is judged inappropriate, it can sometimes be consciously suppressed.

To suppress a feeling is to recognize its presence, take it into account, and then lessen some of its effects. For instance, some people experience a feeling of guilt in the face of any kind of sexual activity, even that which is absolutely legitimate. Repressing such a feeling is liable to bring on psychological phenomena such as frigidity or impotence.

Suppressing a feeling of guilt consists in recognizing that one suffers from it, that it is not rational and that it doubtless comes from an inadequate education. What must be done is to modify it little by little. People should not be surprised that this is not an easy task. If one cannot eliminate guilt feelings, it is useless to become irritated or vexed with oneself. It is often best simply to look upon oneself and one's problem with a benevolent smile. We must, however, be prudent about suppressing a feeling of guilt too quickly since such feelings warn us of some danger. It would be foolish to disconnect a warning bell thoughtlessly. The danger it is signaling may be unreal, but there is always the possibility that the danger is real without our being aware of it. An instinctive reaction can warn us that something is not right. So it happens that even after thinking we have made an excellent decision we can still experience guilt feelings. It is good at such a moment carefully to re-examine the entire question, perhaps with the aid of a capable counselor. He can help discover the various meanings of an action or the implications of guilt feelings.

In any case, guilt feelings liberate a certain psychic energy within us which we must know how to use with an eye to the future. These feelings owe their strength to a conditioning in the past. If the psychic energy stored within them remains fixed in the past, it produces regret and the feelings become complex. Psychological development then remains at the level of "alert" without being able to respond in an appropriate manner. A kind of sterile self–punishment which is called "remorse" may result. If this energy can be directed toward the future, and its point of application made the human group and not the isolated self, remorse becomes repentance and develops into concern and responsibility. The liberated energy will then be used for the purpose of growth, progress, and reintegration.

The moral life of a man will evolve in different fashions according to the manner in which the Oedipal conflict is resolved. If he succeeds in a healthy resolution of the conflict, if he manages to go beyond the stage of competition with his father and becomes his friend, it is possible for him to develop an ethic of encounter.

But if a young man has the persistent impression that he is still his father's rival, he will, as a result, be afraid to develop. His actions, his emotions, his development will seem to him to be a refusal to accept the authority of the father, and he will feel guilty. In this case, the young man, or even the adult, will live constantly under the oppression of the image of his father. He will be made to feel guilty by the repressed desire to "kill his father," and this will lead him to reject all authority. In such a situation, morality often seems a fetter and the growth of the man takes place in opposition to authority. This is actually a morality of the superego in which the law appears as a law of terror. We find ourselves, then, in the presence of what we recognized at the phenomenological level as an ethic of taboo or prohibition. At the worst, the presence of authority will make the adult "regress" in an effort to find in his own past a way of living out this situation in a tolerable way. No adult moral development is possible in this framework.

Two typical reactions characterize this regression: (1) taking refuge in norms; this is a regressive attitude in which one tries to find a solution to the problems of life in an established rule or in an authority which one fears. Basically, this is a flight from giving the ego all of its full responsibility because one does not dare to do so, and (2) revolting against all norms; this is a regressive attitude by which a man puts himself into an equally infantile framework by a perpetual and unproductive rebellion against all authority figures. This framework is no longer the one of convenient submission, but that of systematic affirmation of the self. Such an irrational attitude is evidenced by the revolt against all norms which characterize some political thought and the dynamics of some groups. It is what the Marxists term a "leftist deviation." Such a revolt is more a burden which crushes the rebel than a practical, producive attitude.

The fear of paternal authority or the fear of norms can just as well manifest itself as an uncompromising conservatism and an expressed need for security measures. Continually finding fault with the actions of others often shows fear of the law rather than a genuine concern about morals. Doing "one's own thing" at any cost can also be an attempt to insist on one's freedom while still fearing the law, thereby actually being unfree. The common denominator in all these regressive reactions is that it is the id and the superego which are directing the person's reactions. Man's activity is still not self–directed: he is the slave of his own conflicts.

In order to develop a morality freed from the element of "terror" which characterizes a less-than-adult maturity, we must see the possibilities for human behavior and structured activity when man seeks to give meaning to his life. There are two possible ways man can react to his environment: passively and creatively. These two ways of response can be captured in the images of *the nomad* and *the pioneer*.

Nomads drift from one oasis to another. Having no stable place to live, they are always dependent on their environment. When the chief assembles his subjects and tells them that they are leaving for the next oasis, there is only the appearance of a decision; in fact nature has already made that decision for them. There is no more grass in that particular oasis. They are, in truth, forced to leave. In reality, not even the chief himself has made the decision; staying would mean starvation. Since the nomads have not decided to change their environment, they have submitted to it and are obliged to obey it. Thus, the liberty they enjoy is more imaginary than real; they simply have no alternative.

There are many people who are nomads. They do nothing but react to the stimuli of the surrounding situation. They do not change it. We can see nomads on the university level. As students, they passively accept the demands of the academic establishment. They work for exams and come away with a degree, enslaved to the administrative routine. The same kind of people are to be found in business and industry. They change nothing of the routine that stifles them. Though they perhaps strongly criticize "the system" and so express a certain caricature of real liberty, they lack the imagination or the courage to change it. They do not have within themselves the resources to transform their surroundings.

Pioneers function in a different manner. When they arrive in a place, they make the decision to transform their new environment. They irrigate the soil, cultivate the fields, construct dikes; they "humanize" their environment. They invest in the surrounding situation and that investment bears fruit.

Having sufficiently controlled their environment, they can now choose what they want to do. Each situation presents several alternatives. It is no longer nature that obliges them to leave or to stay, for their decisions are really free ones. What they have accomplished becomes for them a principle of liberty.

There are pioneers everywhere. They are those who choose to transform the environment in which they live in order to remain free. At the university, they are the students who do not simply endure the system, but use it to further their personal formation. In business and industry, they alter the day–to–day routine in order to reach objectives that they themselves have determined. Pioneers, too, criticize "the system," but it is not mere words or vain imagining; it becomes real action. To be a pioneer is to accept the reality principle. The man himself makes his life meaningful. The pioneer gives himself sufficiently stable roots so that he can be himself as he integrates the demands of reality and dominates them.

There are, then, those persons who let themselves be passively manipulated by environmental stresses, and those who accept reality with the intention to structure their own activity and the forces surrounding them. Some people approach life as nomads, victims of their environment. Others approach life as pioneers, determined to be creators of their environment and refusing to be mere victims. Nomads can sometimes live under the guise of pioneers, and vice-versa.

We sometimes mistake for a pioneer the person who has a settled life which can be called "middle class." The middle–class man is settled—he has arrived. In order to get there, he has transformed his environment and made a place for himself. But make no mistake; he is simply a sedentary nomad continuing a routine and continuing to live as he has always done. He has stopped transforming his environment and has become, while remaining where he is, a true nomad. We all meet people like this, people who are successful in life but who can no longer open themselves to others and who are afraid to make new things happen.

It is interesting to note too that a true pioneer can be hidden under the appearance of a nomad. Such, for example, are the "realistic revolutionaries," those who have no place to settle, who move from place to place, often living in a hostile environment but who also transform their environment continually. These people perhaps may seem rather unstable in the eyes of the establishment. Yet men like Gandhi, Mao Tse-Tung, Lenin, Martin Luther King, and Francis of Assisi were all true pioneers. They transformed their environment, acquiring a certain kind of liberty through their actions, though often painfully and at the price of much effort. They were, truly, more free than all those who passively accept the slavery of the established order.

Note that nomads are very rarely happy people. Little by little their lack of real liberty begins to weigh heavily on them. They realize that they are not truly free. The prime example of this slavish nomadism is the drug addict. In the end he is totally dependent on the drug. He has completely abandoned the active creation of his liberty. His life is no longer his own since he is completely submerged in an imaginary world.

Recently the West has given birth to a special kind of nomad, namely, the slave of performance. We see this in people who are totally enslaved in creating the "good life" —as it is defined by our consumer society. Marcuse wonders whether our whole Western civilization, centered as it is on production and consumption has not become enslaved by this tendency. Has real liberty become impossible in our society, leaving to contemporary man simply the illusory liberty to work and to consume? While thinking of himself as a pioneer, as a creator of society, man has become rather, the slave of his socio-economic systems, a victim of his technologized environment.

The task now is to develop a way of living a moral life. To do so, two possible methods might be used. One systematically develops a philosophical ethic and the other simply gives the results. The first examines how and under what conditions human activity can realize its full meaning. This method has the advantage of being highly structured; its only inconvenience lies in its abstract character. In the following chapters, we will use the second method, offering the "results" of a search and a vision. Hopefully the coherence and power of these reflections will themselves be creative of meaning for life. This "method," like that of Teilhard de Chardin, consists in developing a way of looking at reality which is liberating. Hopefully, it provides an opportunity for people to enlarge their vision of the world.

These reflections take their inspiration from Christian tradition and terminology. Nevertheless we think this particular terminology corresponds to the experience of moral life expressed in other traditions, both religious and non–religious.

For Further Reading

Frankl, Viktor E., *Man's Search for Meaning,* Ilse Lasch, trans. (Boston: Beacon Press, 1963).

> The story of a psychiatrist's experience in a concentration camp. Dr. Frankl's conclusion is that finding a meaning to life is more important than any other factor in the achievement of happiness.

Hall, E. T., *The Silent Language* (Garden City, N.Y.: Doubleday & Co., 1959).

> This is a tremendous little book which is especially valuable for its contributon to increasing awareness that any one particular culture and its values is but one among many and will, at times, have to bear the label, "different."

Lee, Dorothy, "Culture and the Experience of Value" in *New Knowledge in Human Values,* Abraham H. Maslow, ed. (New York: Harper & Row, 1959).

> A fascinating article describing the influence of culture on the perception of values.

Maslow, Abraham H., *Motivation and Personality* (New York: Harper & Row, 1970).

> A very useful presentation of the hierarchy of needs and wants within the context of human behavior.

CHAPTER III

LOVE, JUSTICE, AND FORGIVENESS

A liberating vision can be perceived in the words of Christ:" You shall love God with your whole heart, with your whole soul, and your neighbor as yourself; in this double commandment is the whole of the law." This perspective harmonizes two aspects of love. He who turns toward the other encounters in him a reality which is more than human. The love of others has a transcendent dimension. The Christian sees the very presence of God in the love of the "neighbor"; the other reflects The Other. This is not however an exclusive prerogative of Christianity; other philosophical or religious systems have also expressed this transcendent aspect of human life in different terms.

According to St. John it is essential to the meaning of human life that love came to us before we were able to love. God, he says, has loved man first. What "was in the beginning" was not a threat, but love, and perfect love, as St. John affirms, casts out fear. To accept the reality of such a love prior to response means assuming an attitude of acceptance and receptivity toward life. It means opening oneself to love. Such an attitude is not acquisitive or anxious. It is the discovery of the profound liberty of one who knows that he is loved. It means, as we shall see, the triumph of joy, peace, and love over fear.

41

Primarily, then loving is neither performing deeds nor wanting to possess the other, but, accepting to be loved. To be accepting and receptive in this way is to "de-center" oneself and to discover that we are valuable because we are loved. It is living in the presence of another, considering him as the one who frees us because he shows us that we are worthwhile and lovable. The first condition of love, then, is to let oneself be liberated by others and to grant the priority of loving to the other.

But once one has accepted to be loved, the situation reverses itself. When one persons opens himself to another, he also gives that other the power to become liberated too. So each is liberated by the other and gives the other the possibility of liberating himself. For such a situation to exist, a man must drop all his defenses, all the walls he has built around himself to prevent others from reaching him, from "touching" him. This, obviously, does not happen at once but is an on-going process.

The acceptance of love leaves one vulnerable. Accepting love means letting oneself be "touched." The very word has a double meaning which is significant within the context of our discussion. To be "touched" is to leave one's own solitude and let oneself be reached by others. This can be understood in both a physical and a psychological sense.

To keep up his psychological defenses a man must maintain a certain *physical* distance from others. What makes love love, is that one lets one's body be touched and that this physical contact is not an intrusion but the trusting welcome of the approach of the other. In the figurative sense, people do not like to let themselves be "touched" (i.e., emotionally moved) because they are afraid of the other. Allowing oneself to be "touched" by someone means becoming vulnerable and granting the other some power over oneself. In the literal sense, we find the same fear of physical contact. It is another type of defense which an accepting love will drop. The acceptance of physical love implies both a decrease of fear of the other and a growth of trust in him. Aggressiveness toward the other person disappears in this kind of trust.

At both levels, literal and figurative, a similar tension appears. Each person has a zone of defense (psychological or physical) around him. Opening oneself to the other means choosing to live, not behind "defense lines" but "in the open," outside oneself. Therefore, the statement of St. John that "God loved us first" does not simply describe an intellectual insight. On the contrary, it reveals a whole way of looking at life. For St. John, it is basic that there is a love which reaches us first so that it is possible for us to dare make ourselves vulnerable, to begin to love.

At this level of our reflection, we see morality as accepting to be loved and loving in reurn. But it is important to realize that this love must be authentic. It must be a liberating love, a love which makes a person more "himself" so that his actions flow from what is deepest in him. For loving is very different from possessing. Loving means accepting the other as he is, but also wanting him to grow. This openness toward a "more" does not necessarily know what that "more" will be, but expects it nevertheless. We see that love implies some hope in the other's changing. One hopes that the beloved will become better or that he will develop totally. But even if no growth is forthcoming, true love remains absolutely trusting in spite of all. This already indicates that we are not speaking of just any kind of love.

Is it possible, then, to speak of a "code" or law of morality which might indicate how authentic love is usually defined?

There can be a "code of morality," but only in the sense that it be the elaboration of the first and only moral law, that of the acceptance of being loved and of loving in return. This code calls for precepts which expresses what "loving" really means in a given culture at a given time.

But this code has meaning only insofar as it is related to the law of love. Something is immoral only if it contradicts the law of love. A moral precept which is not an expression of the law of love is not an authentic moral precept at all.

The role of precepts is educative; they show people how to express love. Morality as the apprenticeship of love calls for a whole education. It seems clear, for instance, that many people can not develop and grow in adult love unless they are educated in sexual morality. Sexual morality can point out how one might integrate one's sexuality in order to live the law of love. The value of moral precepts comes from their challenge to us. Thanks to them we can discover what demands love makes of us. If there are no norms or if society does not elaborate a moral law, it is quite difficult for people to learn how to love. When a precept seems quite abnormal to us (when we do not see how it expresses the law of love), that can mean one of two things: either that the precept is useless and inauthentic (it does not express the law of love), or that it shows us there is yet a gap between the way we envisage love and what authentic love really is. For the latter case, the precept is really fulfilling its proper role. For many situations, there is a mixture of both cases: the precept is partly useless, and we are not loving authentically.

It must be stressed that moral precepts are only valid to the extent that they really express what it means to love. Thus, for example, suicide is an evil insofar as it is a refusal to experience one's own life, to cope with the difficulties of existence. In the long run, it is a refusal to love. But, if suicide becomes for someone a way of coping with life or of truly loving, it becomes perhaps a "sacrifice" rather than a cowardly act. At this point the absolute nature of this moral law must be reconsidered. Likewise, in a problem such as birth control, we must look for the authentic expression of love. It is not a question simply of wanting to know whether or not one can "use the pill" but of seeking "what best expresses love," and how that love involves more than just the relationship between a man and a woman.

The law, then, is a kind of codification of the "way of love." But if it is characterized only in this manner, there is the risk of misunderstanding the nature of love and the implication of justice that it contains. This distinction between the law of justice and the law of love is significant.

In society there are two kinds of relationships among men: those based on the fact that men are one, and those based on the fact that men are different. This second type of relationship carries with it the obligation of being "just" toward the other, that is, of respecting him insofar as he is different from me. Before striving for unity among men, we must know how to accept dissimilarity. Justice explains what should be done in order to respect this dissimilarity.

Normally it is rather hypocritical to speak of friendship at the very beginning of a relationship. Before I can be the bartender's friend, I must pay for the glass of beer I am drinking; before the professor and the student can be friends, they must accept their respective roles of professor and student. A relationship should always begin with justice, i.e., with respect for certain dissimilarities; then and only then can the parties become friends. The demands of justice must be fulfilled first so that disinterested love can follow. When the difference beween persons is recognized, the access to love is open.

Although the law of justice does not directly express the law of love, it mediates it. It is an expression of the law of love insofar as justice must first be respected in order to love. This distinction between the realities of love and justice is essential, for it expresses a deep insight concerning human life. Man does not live alone; other men exist also. Justice not only allows man to distinguish between love and intrusion, but also to affirm each man's unique dignity. By the law of justice, society decides what a just contract is; without such a law, a contract could become an act of aggression. (Whether this takes form in written or unwritten laws these are always relative to the culture in which they are expressed.)

Justice can be denied in a too rigid structuring of life as well as negligence of any structure at all. Typical examples are economic paternalism and some hippie communes. Paternalism attempts to apply the law of love before fulfilling the demands of justice; it undermines the law of justice by pretending to give, in love, what should first of all be given in justice. The history of Belgium and the Congo demonstrate economic paternalism. As for some hippie communities, by refusing all structure, they want to establish a life of love without first admitting the necessity of being just. Their love then has a hollow sound, for love in the abstract does not usually give rise to concrete deeds.

These questions of how authentic love can be recognized and of how it is based on justice are important ones. A passage from the writings of Dostoyevski indicates in a striking way how an attempt might be made to answer these questions. In *The Brothers Karamazov,* Dostoyevski describes a dialogue between a young anarchist dying of tuberculosis and his old nurse.

> Little one, will you let me light the candle in front of the picture? [In the past he had been against this and would even put it out.] Of course, of course, nanny. I was a monster to forbid you to. You pray by lighting a candle, and I pray, happy that you do so. So both of us, we pray to the same Lord.

This passage clearly describes the several stages found within the dialectic of authentic love.

First, the young man refuses to let his nurse act as she pleases. As he himself says, this is monstrous. Even if what another does is disagreeable or meaningless to me, I cannot

46

force him to do otherwise. The other is free to do what he wants. Note that this is precisely the attitude of the God of Christianity. God wants man to be free; he does not want him to be a slave. He does not want to force him to do anything; he accepts him as he is. The first stage of love, therefore, is to come to the point of allowing the other to be himself. This does not necessarily mean that everything he does is approved, nor that there is not hope of improvement, nor that all attempts to change his mind are abandoned. It is merely the acceptance of the law of justice. No conquest of the other is attempted; he is recognized as having a right to be himself.

Second, "you pray by lighting a candle." This is the acceptance of the existence of real value in the actions and decisions of the other. The young man here recognizes the validity of the nurse's act of lighting the candle; he recognizes the action as she sees it. Perhaps he does not understand it entirely, but he admits that it exists. In this second stage of the structure of love, the value of what the other does is acknowledged, even if this value is somewhat strange to me or even if it challenges me. It is quite obvious that while we recognize the value of another's choice, it does not mean that we are completely satisfied with the situation. Far from it. But it is still important to affirm the worth of another's point of view or action. Although it is possible that we do not really understand this value, by admitting its existence, we accept the limitations of our own point of view and gain a better view of reality.

Third, "and I pray, too, happy that you do so." When we accept another; when we are happy that he is himself (even if he is different), then we participate in the goodness of what he does. The young man says, "I pray." He shares in what is good in the nurse's action because he is happy that she does it. This is already love; now we are beyond justice. Obviously, this third stage presupposes a mutual effort to overlook the deficiencies of the other. It even implies the acceptance of the "faults" or blunders of the other. Wishing the other to be free and accepting him as he is (even in the very pain this may bring) is the beginning of love. It is a love which opens the way to a hope for the solution of difficulties.

Fourth, the young man says further: ". . . both of us, we pray to the same Lord." The just recognition of the fact that he and his nurse possess distinct individualities has opened the young man to a new dimension. He discovers in this fourth stage, in some way, they are both caught up in a single movement. Accepting the other as different, accepting love, has opened him to a much fuller life and a depth of union in differences. In fact, if the analysis were pursued a little further, it might be discovered that the love which has so developed as a participation in a more absolute love which tradition has called "God."

We submit that every encounter which leads to growth in love follows this fourfold process of *acknowledgement of the law of justice* (letting the other be and not interfering with him), *attainment of a deeper insight into the law of justice* (accepting the other in appreciating his values), *initiation into the law of love* (being happy with, and, in a certain way, entering into the values of the other), and *discovery of a new dimension* (the realization of the existence of individual freedoms and a force which unites them in a single dynamism implying growth for each). But nowhere is this process more striking than in the encounter of two political adversaries who want to fulfill the ultimate expectation of love: the love of enemies. The dynamism of this love can be described as follows: First, recognizing the adversary and letting him say what he wants to say: this is justice. Second, recognizing that he, too, desires the common good: this is still justice. This recognition already unites the two political adversaries in a single goal, the common good they

48

both desire. Third, being happy that the other also wants the common good; this is already a beginning of union in love. Fourth, recognizing that adversaries are united in a single movement which transcends them. This means the splitting of the narrow framework of political conflict in order to be open to a deeper love. This love, however, does not preclude the existence of painful struggle even if we assume there will be a true reconciliation. Non-loving or non-moral attitudes stop before the end of this development. The refusal to love "unto the end" may reside in the withdrawal from necessary confrontation with the other, just as well as in the refusal to love him at all.

The process which we have described above is Dostoyevski's "attitude of humble love." It is humble love which opens the possibility of a truly loving encounter. Through it we discover that each situation is an occasion of growth; that a new dimension has been added to our lives; and that we can break out of the narrowness in which we are prone to enclose ourselves. For Dostoyevski, this dynamism of love is a greater force than violence. It is a force which no other can equal.

There still remains, however, one stumbling block: sin. Man can remain perplexed in the face of sin, the refusal to love. The question arises as to what should be done when we meet such a refusal. Should we reject the other or still try to welcome him in forgiving love? How do we respond to the reality of sin? Do we seek escape or can we appeal to a "higher law"—that of forgiveness?

Among the explanations for the morbid pleasure an individual can take in remorse, there is often found a refusal to allow himself to be loved or even to accept himself as lovable. This may show up as a refusal to hope that "after what I've done," I can still be loved and forgiven. There can be a kind of masochistic enjoyment in remaining intent on one's evil action or in taking pleasure in one's "unworthiness." Remorse sometimes signifies fear: fear of trusting, of letting oneself be touched by the forgiveness of the other. This is really a refusal to change, to again turn toward others. In the end, solitude is preferred to forgiveness. If, on the contrary, forgiveness is preferred to solitude, a new lease on life begins.

Any relationship which would not include the element of forgiveness (both given and received) is liable not to be rooted in reality and so remains superficial. Indeed, as long as we have not admitted that we must forgive each other our limitations, we have not yet encountered one another. Forgiveness brings a new depth to the relationship. "If I have sinned against all," says Dostoyevski in *The Brothers Karamazov*, "then all will forgive me. That is heaven." "The very fault that others have committed against us," says Louis Lavelle, "creates between us and them a bond of flesh which forgiveness makes spiritual."

When we are honest with ourselves, i.e., when we try to be "authentic," we have to admit that our relationships with others are often barely human. Most of the time we live in what Heidegger has called the impersonal world of "they"; the "run-of-the-mill" world in which man lives side-by-side with his neighbor without really being aware of him. It is a world in which we treat each other more like things than persons. It is the world of indifference.

What often tears us out of this kind of existence is precisely the world of indifference.

What often tears us out of this kind of existence is precisely the wound that the other inflicts upon us. Whether we suffer because he treats us like a "thing" or because, for one reason or another, he hurts us, he has still "gotten to us." To speak of encounter without admitting that there exist failings in our communion, suggests we are not yet living on the level of real personal encounter. Confronted with suffering and pain, we can see more clearly in what way and to what extent our lives are linked. There is a bond of flesh between us. When this is realized, each feels he is a human being and hopes that life may be other than existence on the level of "they." For those who leave themselves open to it, suffering introduces into life the dimension of the "I" and the "Thou."

Perhaps, then, the crucial question in life is "What response do we give in the face of suffering?"

There is, first, the violent response of hate. Hate establishes between persons a bond much deeper than that of indifference. But it is a bond between opponents and one can always quit the game. In an attempt to avoid fault, man is often tempted to isolate himself from others and set himself up as a "just man" outside the communion of sinners. But it is an impossible attempt. Not only does honesty oblige us to admit that we are not "just," but any attempt to isolate ourself as "just" only intensifies the divisions among men. Is there another way?

Dostoyevski sums up his answer—an answer which is that of the whole Christian tradition—in this way: "There is only one possible salvation: to take upon oneself all the sins of men." This is the only way to accept being among men and foster their unity. It is what Dostoyevski called "humble love" and the "greatest force in the world." It is the way of forgiveness. The communion created through awareness of fault now becomes a community of forgiveness. That which divided becomes the thing which unites. Men, so united, not only forgive each other personal offenses, but also those unwilled but painful inadequacies. Even offensive characteristics in the other become a source of love for those who are open. This comes not through taking negative morbid pleasure in faults, but through seeing in them the revelation of a person who has entered my life and has touched me.

Openness to a community and to forgiveness offers itself

51

as an obvious answer to the problem of evil. That is what the Christian tradition is all about. Jesus willed to give himself up to men, accepting them as they were; this included the risk of seeing himself killed by them as well as his hope of liberating them. Following his example, Christian tradition invites his disciples to come after him in the way of humble love, accepting perhaps, to be taken where he himself went, namely to death. This attitude carries a practical, not merely a theoretical solution to the problem of evil.

It is important to realize that this humble love is not that unconcerned love which simply "lets things ride." Humble love demands change. Whether he changes or not, the other should always be accepted. But love is also hope and invitation. It is a hope that leads to action in view of a better world. Finally, humble love is founded on the conviction that ultimately no one can either destroy a free man or keep him from loving. Everything, even the negative attitude of the other, can be integrated into a new love.

If one lives in attitude of total openness to the other, he cannot come to harm. Very often, though, out of a very understandable fear, a man surrounds himself with defenses. When he is faced with the possibility of a real encounter, he goes back into his shell; he regresses. He fails to see that even in the most alienating situations, there is the possibility of progress, of growth and love. Unfortunately, the very shell in which he takes refuge is also that which keeps him from growing.

It is said that the people who show the most love are also those who accept living without defenses, who do not even feel the need to protect themselves. Far from depleting themselves, sharing with others increases the love in their lives. Emmanuel Mounier expresses it perfectly: "I often dream of a world where one could stop the first passerby at a street corner, and perceive immediately all that he is, entering into that inner dialogue of his with ease and no surprise. The few times that I have met a person of such caliber, as to allow me to take such liberty, I have done so. Thus were born my best friendships."

For Further Reading

Dostoyevski, Fydor, *The Brothers Karamazov.*
In this novel (available in a number of translations), Dostoyevski explores the depths of love, justice, freedom, and forgiveness. His "Legend of the Grand Inquisitor" is one of the most forceful texts on freedom ever written.

PART TWO

AVENUES FOR AN ETHIC
OF HUMAN GROWTH

Chapter IV

ERIKSON'S THEORY OF
THE LIFE-CYCLE

The psychologist Erik Erikson describes the cycles of life involved in the growth into adulthood. These cycles sketch the various stages a man goes through in his maturation process. Obviously, these cycles should not be taken too literally nor should it be thought that they describe the process in all its details. They are rather a convenient manner of speaking and useful only insofar as they help us to gain a better understanding of how a human being develops. A cycle is never completed. Each stage revives what was experienced in those stages that preceded it and previous "crises of growth" are re-experienced on a different level.

This cyclic growth has various ethical implications. Since at each stage of life the personality is structured in a different way, the law of love and of charity manifests its demands differently throughout a lifetime. It is important to investigate the significance of the crises and ambiguities of each cycle of life since they comprise a growth toward a greater love. Erikson distinguishes eight cycles of four components each. While this presentation closely follows Erikson's own thought, a fifth component will be added suggesting the religious implications of each life cycle.

The components of each cycle are:

First, an emotional change: when a man passes from one stage to another, his relationship to society changes, effecting a psychological crisis, the solution of which brings into play a new force or a new way of living social relationships. We can call this the specific psycho-social energy evoked. Second, a certain ambivalence: the uneasiness experienced at the beginning of a new stage may be linked with psychopathological elements. Third, societal implications: individual growth is related to certain institutions of society. Fourth, development of values: each cycle calls for and promotes a particular virtue. And, fifth, religious aspects: the individual's religious insight follows this overall development and can take on either negative or positive forms. Each stage involves some religious ambiguity in which religious attitudes can develop in one of two directions: one healthy and progressive; the other unhealthy and regressive. We will present the religious development from a Christian viewpoint.[1]

First Cycle—Infancy: Trust Versus Mistrust: Hope

The resolution of a man's initial psycho-social crisis is primarily dependent on the interaction of mother and infant. The mother must, in all her behavior, give the infant almost physical proof that she is "faithful" and "trustworthy." The infant can then experience in a personal way that the world in which he lives can be good for him and fulfill his own needs. It is a reciprocal relationship since the infant evokes hope in her and others and helps her develop confidence. In this way the child awakens in adults an

1 When we present the "Christian viewpoint," it should be understood that we are presenting Christian theology as we understand it. There are other theological views and our interpretation on some point is certainly open to debate. Nonetheless, the purpose of this book is not theological. We will simply present one viewpoint without taking time to justify it or defend it.

energy which corresponds to the experience of "responsibility" (see Seventh Cycle). Through this interaction the child, too, experiences "hope." It is a primary and essential force which will give the full-grown person a kind of instinctive certainty that he can trust his environment and the people around him.

The suffering inevitable in the delay of immediate satisfactions which weaning and growth imply can give the infant the impression of being abandoned and provoke him to desperate rage. This tension is produced by the impression of being forsaken, and will often reappear in adult life. In difficult moments, the strength to hope may depend in part on the trust which a person's mother was able to inspire in the infant at a very early age. A lack of this fundamental trust may show up in childhood or adolescent neuroses. It may also emerge later, e.g., in drug addicts or those who withdraw into psychotic states. It seems to them that their whole world has abandoned them and so they "drop out" of it.

The interaction between mother and infant is fundamental to three very important feelings in society: First, the experience which the child, if a girl, will use later on when she is a mother herself. Second, a feeling of oneness with the world: "you can count on it"; the environment is not hostile. In his responsibilities, the future adult will not be isolated from others or from the world. Third, a convincing conception of "providence." At this psychological level, the function of "providence" is to give expression to the fact that in any situation there is room for hope.

These feelings are often manifested in an organized religion which celebrates in its rites a reconciliation which relies upon hope.

Hope is therefore the essential psycho-social force of this first cycle of growth. It is the solid belief that one will be able to realize one's basic desires in spite of the anarchy of drives and the rage provoked by the feeling of dependence.

At the religious level, it follows that it is the image of an all–provident God which appears at this stage of growth. This image of a god, conceived as maternal, can be deformed. This happens if the divinity is presented as a god who does not care about men and who leaves them to their helplessness. But it can be just as deformed if it is presented as a god who constantly intervenes in man's life in order to satisfy all his needs. This latter "god" would strongly resemble an over–protective mother. An adult who has not "grown out" of this will behave in such a way as to never oppose what he believes to be the wishes of the divinity (or of others). Expressions like "not to displease God" may contain overtones of such feeling. In the face of this deviation which would keep a person from being fully himself, the Christian doctrine of providence does not seem to say that everything that happens is necessarily willed by God, but rather that in every situation people are being called and that they can determine their own free response. The situation in which man is placed may very well be the result of evil which God himself cannot eliminate without making simple puppets of us. Christian theology declares nonetheless that in the actual situation, we can open ourselves to the future; this hope is based on the love of God for us. God loves us and calls us in each event of our life.

Second Cycle—Early Childhood; Autonomy Versus the Face of Shame and Doubt: Will

At this point in his development, the child acquires a certain psycho-social autonomy. He begins to master his body. He can walk, talk, recognize certain categories such as "yes and no," "good and bad," "just and unjust," "mine and yours." At this stage, the awareness of being made more on his own makes the child realize that he can do even more: that he can control himself. The sense of self–control which brings with it a certain self–esteem is the origin of a sense of free–will in the individual. If, however, the child feels dominated from without and not appreciated, he is liable to experience shame and doubt.

Shame is the disturbing emotion which is aroused by the awareness of being exposed to the look of others. One would like to bury oneself, hide or sink into the ground. Vulnerability to shame is exploited all through life by certain cultures; they are quick to blame and shame the members of the society. This feeling can be so strong that it produces the desire of suicide as a way of "disappearing." Closely related to shame is doubt; an unsureness of one's own will. There are some people who are so unsure of themselves that they feel they have no alternative but to accept every judgment or order of others. But there are also those who mistrust every opinion. So there are the "yes-men" on the one hand and the confirmed rebels on the other; neither type knows how to escape from the feeling of being criticized. This feeling even goes so far as to produce compulsive neuroses or paranoid fears which see hidden critics and disguised persecutors everywhere. It can also be expressed by the fear of having to submit to something no matter what.

The autonomy of the will exhibited in early childhood does not develop at random; it has both structures and limits. There are social institutions corresponding to this feeling of autonomy: order, law, and justice. These institutions are for people and not for themselves; people, however, who constantly doubt themselves will prefer to think of these institutions as absolutely objective and inflexible; they will then be perceived as oppressive and will not be taken for their functional value.

The *will*, thus, is the firm determination to exercise free choice as well as to act as one sees fit, in spite of the unavoidable experiences of shame, doubt, and a certain anger at being controlled by others. "Good will" can be seen, then, as basic to the acceptance of law and of circumstances. It will will be rooted in the good judgment of parents guided by the spirit of the law.

At the religious level, there can be a number of deviations by which man uses "God" to avoid making his own decisions. Thus, God is often presented as one who arouses shame in man. Before him, some say, we should "bury ourselves" in shame; we should trust him to the point of not trusting in ourselves at all. This is a caricature of humility and is, in fact, nothing else but a rationalization of the feelings of shame and of doubt in the person who does not know how to accept his autonomy. In the end, God is presented as someone who intimates to us that we should reject ourselves.

This deformation of religious sentiment is contrary to the most authentic Christian tradition. God has loved us first. There is no reason for fear or shame before him. On the contrary, it is he who comes to us as the liberator of the poor, the oppressed, the lowly. Consequently, trust in God, far from leading us to mistrust ourselves or to reject our own autonomy, leads us to the discovery of what we really can do. St. Ignatius Loyola put it well when he said: "We must believe in God in such a way that we work as if everything depended on us." By this he meant that faith in God should make us discover a person who wants us to be ourselves. God is not one who makes us feel we would like to "sink into the ground." Thanks to him, man feels the courage to stand up straight.

Third Cycle—The Oedipal Stage; Initiative Versus Guilt: The Decision to Act

Capable of independent movement, the three- to four-year-old child is ready to understand the roles he is expected to assume. He begins to play and to imitate adults and so develops his sense of initiative as well. He now associates with those of his own age and his games become matters of import. He not only enjoys them but they are the means of his accomplishing something. He develops his still–limited capacities, begins to conceptualize and tries to fit his newly found world of symbols into both interior and exterior reality. He begins to be aware of the way in which he can act upon this reality.

The emerging conscience of the child brings with it a new ambivalence. An interior voice tells him what to do. This "monitor" watches, judges, and sometimes punishes him. The child feels ill at ease; sometimes he even experiences a kind of guilt feeling in setting a goal for himself, initiating or accomplishing something (or even just imagining it). Among his peers he discovers competition. In his family, he encounters the Oedipus conflict. He feels like his father's rival, and this gives him a feeling of guilt. This sense of guilt can produce in the child a complex which paralyzes his action. He feels inhibited and timid. For the adult, pathological expressions of the conflict will appear in a denial of potentialities; fear of action; the presence of impotence or frigidity. It can also express itself as exhibitionism or the need to continually act out a role. But if the crisis is overcome, the child will enter a world of action.

In the societal context, that action produces what we might call an "enterprising spirit." Assuming this, society can build a certain "ethic of action." This ethic will determine the technological and cultural objectives the child and future adult must attain. These will sometimes be incorporated into religious rituals which actualize the meaning and the necessity of action.

The *decision to act* is the courage to envisage and pursue valid and tangible goals, guided by conscience, but not paralyzed by feelings of guilt or fear of punishment.

It is well–known that this stage of life includes tension

regarding parental authority. This ambiguity is liable to affect the concept of God as father. Man may begin to consider God as a rival. He relives, as it were, the unsatisfactorily resolved rivalry with his own father. People sometimes say: "I would have liked to have done something with my life, but God won out and, for better or worse, this is where I am today." If such an admission can express how the transcendent sometimes changes our life, it seems questionable if it implies that the transcendent wants to direct and oppress our life. Another way of deforming the concept of God is by making him the custodian of morality. God becomes *the authority figure*; he decrees what is good and what is evil; he condemns and punishes. Christian theology will not support these conceptions of God. God never competes with his own creatures; he did not come to condemn them but to liberate them. The Christian concept of God as "judge" must not be understood in the setting of a tribunal before which man is to be called. In both the Old and New Testaments, the judge is presented as someone rich and powerful, who comes to save the poor man, the sinner and the wretched one. The "just" man (in the bad sense of the word) needs no judge because he is capable of protecting his own rights, or believes himself to be. But the poor man, the orphan, the widow all need someone who will safeguard their interests. They need a judge who will give them the human dignity which an unjust society has perhaps stolen from them. The "judgment" of God brings the real situation to light and shows what a man really is, beneath exterior success or failure. The Christian concept of God as authority is at the opposite pole of these deformations. At The Last Supper, Jesus called his disciples not "servants" but "friends."

Fourth Cycle—The Fully Developed Child; Skill Versus Inferiority: Competence

As the child develops his skills, he acquires a degree of competence in certain techniques which he will need in his culture. Through the process of becoming absorbed in this new undertaking, he becomes an active member of society; he is integrated into a new group which we call "school." Little by little, school is substituted for play. Some kind of systematic instruction is part of a child's development in all cultures.

The danger at this stage lies in the feeling of inadequacy that the child may experience. If he is doubtful of his skills or his social integration in the presence of his peers, he may despair of ever learning. He may then regress and relive the experience of rivalry typical of the Oedipal period of life. It is at this time that the child's associations within broader groups become important. It is here that he will be introduced to roles which prepare him for his own in business or industry. Thus, youth groups complete the work of the school. He may discover, however, that within such groups the color of his skin or the ethnic or economic background of his parents decide his worth more than his own incentive. Because of this, he may feel unworthy and inferior to others and so have his development stunted by his own society. The child runs the risk, too, of conforming mechanically to what is asked of him in his work. This happens when conformity is the only criterion of value. He may easily sacrifice his own imagination, his spontaneity, his dreams for what is expected of him. He is liable then to become a "mechanical man," a slave of technology or his social position.

This stage of development is also very important for the child's entrance into social life. There is an awareness of the moral value the culture places upon certain skills. So, as the child becomes an active member of the culture, that culture seems to affirm his own worth.

Competence, the basis for active collaboration in the cultural life of a society, is thus the free exercise of ingenuity and intelligence in the accomplishment of meaningful tasks —that is, unimpaired by any infantile sense of inferiority.

Certain religious ideas correspond to this stage of formation. Taken positively, they reveal a God who finds very important to him the men he created—"God really needs men." But the same ideas can also be a reflection of a psychological deformation. That happens when a person finds himself before a God who finds him of no value. This god takes all responsibilities upon himself; man is reduced to a purely passive role. At the extreme, human life would consist simply of accomplishing a plan established by God beforehand. Some people actually conceive the notion of "vocation" in this way; they believe that God dictates to them what they are to do, and they find their security in always carrying it out. Their lives are reduced to a task to be done day–by–day, adding nothing personal to the program. But God has no pre-established plan for our lives. He leaves us free to determine it ourselves. Peguy perceived this with his usual incisiveness when he described God as always looking forward to (and even showing surprise at) the new discoveries of his creatures. In such a religious climate, man can find his fulfillment in the development of his capabilities. In the deviations we have mentioned, he is liable to remain a perpetual minor incapable of asserting himself.

Fifth Cycle—Adolescence; Identity Versus Role Confusion: Fidelity

Having more or less mastered his potentialities and his skills, the child, with the onset of puberty, enters into a new stage. As an adolescent he will be faced with a twofold exigency: he must handle the interior revolution of puberty and, at the same time, prepare for the tasks which the adult world will demand of him. Before those demands, he is above all concerned with his psycho-social identity. He is preoccupied with the question of how he will use his still rudimentary talents and skills and whether or not he can succeed in his future occupation. The discovery of his identity is more than the sum of the identifications he made previously. It is actually the trust he has gained in his own emerging personality. This trust now enables him to come to grips with life.

A sizeable number of tensions are discernible at this stage. The adolescent does not feel really adjusted to his situation. This awkwardness may even lead him to psycho-pathological regressions. And, if, over and above the personal tensions, the adolescent is bewildered by the conflicting roles imposed upon him, his situation may become rather desperate. It is not surprising that depression is common at this age.

The adolescent is looking for a way to take his place and set his life-style among adults. He seeks his identity for reasons which are ideological as much as practical. He searches for interior unity and a set of values that will endure. He wants to develop all his potentialities. This will include either the use of sexual vitality (or its sublimation) in such a way that he will be recognized as a young adult. He is concerned about the image he projects to those whom he admires. Adolescent crushes are attempts to find one's identity by discovering it in an idealized other or in an erotic thrill. Adolescents may also seek a pseudo-identity by forming gangs, by stereotyping their heroes, their idols or even their enemies. At this point, the adolescent is liable to be clanish and cruel by excluding all those who are different from him. The world is divided into "good" and "bad" guys. If the adolescent turns against society as a whole, a temporary or prolonged delinquency can result.

These features show how sociologically important adolescence is, both for the adolescent himself as well as for society as a whole. Actually, the adolescent brings to society a revitalization which is necessary for its evolution. Young people enter the society and oblige it to renew itself, sometimes even by a revolutionary challenge.

If adolescence must always be a period of conflict, it can be less turbulent for young people who have the skills necessary to live in the society as it is. In Western countries, for instance, the transition to adulthood will be easier for those who are gifted and competent in technical and economic production. But, moreover, in order to become a balanced adult, an adolescent needs "ideologies." He seeks a unifying inspiration for his life and thoughts and expects teachings, beliefs, and ideals which express the hope that the society will evolve in the best possible way. Society must confirm youth in its hopes. If it does not succeed in offering these hopes, the adolescent will not easily find his identity and will often fall into the deviations mentioned above.

Fidelity can now be seen as the capacity for persevering in the path of one's commitment despite inevitable contradictions and conflicts. This capacity is the cornerstone of an individual's identity and will be inspired and reinforced by the ideals and way of life accepted in the society.

For the adolescent who is a Christian, Jesus Christ becomes a model, a hero, and a friend; one who evokes the response of man and gives it meaning. But there can also be religious deviations during this stage. The adolescent can create for himself a God toward whom no fidelity is possible—a vague and abstract God, a projection of his own confused identity. At the other extreme, he can also imagine God as one who would ask man to set his life in a fixed system of rigid fidelity. Man would then "freeze" what should always remain flexible and fluid. Instead of opening himself to a living God, he would consecrate himself to a system of solidified beliefs. He would limit his loyalty to a church closed in on itself and in the end would identify his "vocation" with a role set once and for all. The Christian, on the contrary, sees God as one who breaks all established systems, who is present beyond all our definitions and all our categories. "For Christ," said St. Paul, "there are no more pagans, nor Jews, nor masters nor slaves, nor men nor women." Jesus Christ, then, becomes someone to whom one can pledge fidelity without being confined to a rigid existence.

Sixth Cycle—The Young Adult; Intimacy Versus Isolation: Love

An awareness of one's own identity allows a person to have the trust necessary to enjoy friendship, love, or any other type of personal encounter. The young adult is now ready to discover what is meant by intimacy and solidarity. He has become able to commit himself in relationships and promises which will possibly demand of him deep sacrifices and painful compromises. The moral values developed at this stage are a kind of prolongation of the ideological structure which he accepted during adolescence and a prolongation of the sense of moral duty which he received during childhood.

True maturity will be evident by the fact that the person is now able to work and love at the same time. The stress must be put on the three words: it is essential to be able to *work and love*. Love should not prevent work, nor vice–versa.

The danger involved at this stage of the life–cycle is that it is possible for the young adult to isolate himself and to avoid any contact which could lead him into an intimate friendship. Or, on the contrary, he could seek a kind of pseudo-intimacy, using any means, hoping to find in flirting or in sex an identity for which he strives but which he still lacks. The person who has not succeeded in overcoming his isolation or who seeks refuge in pseudo-intimacy could find it difficult ever to love and work without letting one interfere with the other. If this happens, he remains in an infantile state and never achieves maturity.

In human beings, over and above the sex drive which is shared with animals, there is a particular phenomenon called "love." The human being attempts to share his identity and to encounter the other in love. If the couple really wants to learn how to love the loving encounter can help overcome the aggressiveness, fear, guilt, and hardness still very often present in young adults. If the couple agree to try to grow in love, what they will gain by the intimacy of their love experience will allow them to live fruitfully within other human relations (whether cooperative, competitive, or productive.) Perhaps it is important to be aware (as we have indicated briefly) that expressions of physical love only acquire their full significance when they are real encounters with the other. Then physical love is no longer a conquest, nor is it aggressive and intruding, and it then no longer awakens fear. Society has institutionalized this loving encounter in engagement and marriage.

The refusal of intimacy brings with it a hardening of heart, a refusal to live with others, an exaggeration of little personal differences. This refusal is liable to foster prejudices and exclusiveness with regard to anything or anyone foreign or unfamiliar. Those who assume the role of "guides" can use such attitudes to provoke wars or political conflicts.

Love is the acceptance of the other and attachment to him, a feeling which is stronger than the antagonisms which necessarily arise from the diversity of functions within a group.

Since the relationship between God and his creatures is always described as a very intimate one, it is not surprising that this cycle reveals great religious wealth, while at the same time presenting ambiguities. It is true that God loves us. Yet we can accept or refuse to respond to that love.

We must point out certain conceptions of God which lead man to repress emotions. In the end, these false conceptions can isolate an individual even if he imagines he has a deep relationship with the divinity. There is a way of using one's relationship with God as a substitute and a compensation for a lack of human relationship. In this case, the victory over isolation would take place only at the imaginary level, and a man would not really be loving. We must also beware of a notion of God as someone who would ask us to give ourselves to him and the others to the point of no longer expecting to be loved ourselves. Such an attitude, under the appearance of oblative love, is actually the refusal to come out of the isolation in which man always risks enclosing himself.

Over and against these ideas, we find in Christianity the affirmation of a God who did not first ask that we love him, but who loved us first. The meaning of Christianity, therefore, is not based (as is sometimes claimed) on love of neighbor, but on the fact that the Christian has first accepted to be loved and then chosen to love in response. It is not, thus, a question of going to the neighbor, but of allowing another to break the isolation in which one is liable to enclose oneself so that one lives in authentic relationships.

God now appears as the one who loves first, that is, the one who first invites us to let him touch us. But it is brotherly love which is the sign that we are in him, that we are really responding to his love for us.

Seventh Cycle—Maturity; Creative Love Versus Stagnation: Care

The adult now wants to build. A "pioneer" and no longer a "nomad," he is responsible for society and life; he must be concerned about it. Creative love first takes its responsibilities toward the next generation and is mainly expressed in procreation and education. But there is also another kind of love which is incarnated in creativity, in productivity, in concern for others and in the taking on of responsibility.

The refusal to become a responsible being can be expressed in multiple ways. There are parents who have no concern for their children; some resign their authority while others refuse to let their children be themselves. These last only want their children to be copies of themselves and so they dominate them. Adults who refuse to take on their creative responsibility are liable to regress to a previous stage. Among the characteristics of such regression, we can mention the more or less obsessive search for pseudo-intimacy and irresponsible sexual activity. Intimacy which does not lead to responsible generativity (whether physical or spiritual) is soon liable to be nothing more than a mask hiding psychological regression. The most serious effects of this flight from responsibility will appear in the succeeding generation. The tensions within the first cycles of life are generally more serious when the previous generation has refused its responsibilities.

The continuity of the human species is maintained in society because of the institutions of marriage and organized work. These institutions provide the security necessary to allow concern for the next generation and to save it from the necessity of facing life in a society full of confusion. But these institutions themselves can become sclerotic and self–enclosed. We then find closed groups, whether families, churches, clans, or nations which see every stranger as an enemy.

Care is the concern for all which has been engendered by love, by necessity, or by accident. Care should ceaselessly go beyond narrowness or egocentricity in order to become involved in reality.

At the religious level, this stage is that of the realization of a true community of love which is open to all. A false religious sentiment can slip into the ambiguities of this life–cycle, too, and God has too many times become the God of a particular and select group. Such a god, when limited to the dimensions of a particular race, people, or church reinforces intolerance and favors religious wars. At a more individual level, we find the god who favors paternalism. This image of the divinity leads a man to take on himself the responsibilities of others. Under the pretext of protecting the common good, religion, or another important value, he no longer recognizes the limit of his own responsibility. At the other extreme is the quietism by which a man tries to throw all his responsibility onto God. Christianity opposes these values and refuses to confine God to one people or one nation. For the Christian, every man is a neighbor; there are no more real strangers. There are no longer pagans or Jews. All men are brothers. In the Christian scheme of things each person is distinct; no one can take responsibility over another. Jesus said it in these words: "Call no man Father or Master or Rabbi, for you are all brothers."

Eighth Cycle–Old Age; Ego Integrity Versus Despair: Wisdom

He who has traversed life comes to old age full of knowledge and experience; his is a sound judgment. If his psychological evolution was a healthy one, he will use this judgment with kindness, benevolence, and hope: this is wisdom. He is confident as he arrives at the "end of his course." Although his physical and intellectual forces decline, he knows he has gathered personal wealth during his life. At the end of his life, he is ready either to assume or (eventually) to give up the role of guide. He is now one of the "sages."

If this evolution is difficult, it will show up in a hidden fear of death. The destiny which limits life is not accepted. Despair then shows that one has found life too short to permit development. In this case, old people are liable to compete with the young. They attempt to continue jobs they can no longer handle. They are unable to accept themselves simply for what they are and keep trying to attain recognition by what they do. When they can no longer do anything in the present, some try to establish their value and their identity in what they have done in the past; they talk endlessly of their past exploits. Bitterness and disgust characterize this despair which can sometimes degenerate into senile depression, hypochondria, or paranoid hate.

The reality of old age and of death must be faced. What is characteristic of the wisdom of old age is reflection on the ultimate end of man. This is what we call "philosophy." In one way or another, one must now face up to all that existence means.

Modern industrial society is also confronted with this and must grapple with a new problem: the increasing number of aged person. Such persons are more deeply confronted with the ultimate goals of life and our society encounters here a serious question which it has not yet resolved. Our society usually defines a man by his productivity, thinking only of what he accomplishes and leaving little room for those who simply *are*. In the church, provision has been made for upholding the value of existence itself through the contemplative religious orders. Even if he works for his living, the contemplative is not defined by his occupation, but by his relationship with God and others. He thus anticipates in a certain way the crisis of the old

74

person who is confronted more directly with the question of the ultimate meaning of existence.

Wisdom, then, is an attitude toward life which is both unpossessive and committed, yet fully aware that this life is limited by death.

In old age the final end of man and the idea of God are quite important. But even here we must still be aware of ambiguities. There is a way of living religion by which a man seeks to flee from the anguish of his own death. In order to avoid that formidable encounter, some persons speak of death only as a rapid passage and a banal event, preceding eventual survival. But for the truly religious man, the confrontation with death, even in hope, is no less a confrontation. Christianity is clear on this point. Before the Resurrection, Jesus Christ lived the anguish, the solitude, and the surrender of death. He asks Christians to follow him in this way. A theology of survival which would avoid taking the cross and death seriously would no longer be Christian.

Conclusion

These cycles of life form the background of man's growth in his environment and ethical life. In studying his psychological maturation, we have discovered that little by little man learns what it is to love and to show himself a responsible member of his community. By resolving the crises he must live through, he integrates new behaviors into his personality. The study of the cycles of life shows how man can learn to love. This will help to clarify some special points which we will now examine, and which are related to the growth of man and his responsibility in society.

The following chapters investigate a certain number of practical moral problems. Each of them individually calls for a full development which is beyond the scope of this work. The questions are quite complex and, in most instances, it is practically impossible to state honestly that one solution is better than another. We simply present some current thinking on the questions. We cannot give all the reasons which make us opt for one particular solution rather than another; in certain cases, we simply present different points of view and only indicate which one seems most appropriate to us. Our purpose is not to determine what is right and what is wrong. Such a point of view assumes that the meaning of action is obvious. Our purpose is rather to indicate the possible significances of an action so that in the more concrete cases the ambiguities of human actions can be unmasked and the kind of behavior which best expresses the law of love and justice can then be found. It is not the task of the ethician to tell people what they should do; he only indicates the consequences of the possible choices.

For Further Reading

Erikson, Erik H., *Identity, Youth and Crisis* (New York: W. W. Norton & Co., 1968).

In this work Erikson offers his description of the life–cycles which is particularly relevant to our study.

CHAPTER V

SEXUALITY, LOVE, PROMISE,
AND FIDELITY

In every culture, the code of sexual morality is very complex and is composed of multiple prohibitions. Some of these have social or psychological roots; others originate from ethical reasons. Only these latter are direct expressions of the law of love and of charity. The others proceed from the psycho-social structures that express a given society's insight concerning morals. In this sense, then, they are not absolute.

In every society, sexuality plays an extremely important part. Not only does it awaken man's deepest emotions, but it constitutes one of the highest forms of human communication. The most stable institutions of a society can only be built on the foundation of sexual relations. Important sociological institutions such as marriage and the education of children are linked with sexuality. It is not surprising that the code of sexual morality is a fairly elaborate one.

In the Christian view, sexual morality has often been represented as a commandment dictated by God or flowing from the "nature of man." Such expressions, which can be justified to some extent, can also, perhaps, give the impression that sexual morality is an arbitrary commandment of God. This is not the case at all. Sexual morality, like the rest of morality, is part of the law of love. The problem of sexual ethics is the problem of how a human being can learn to "love" not only with his mind, but also with his body. Sexuality is at the service of love. Any behavior, then, which is in accord with the law of love is "good"; that which would deter one from this end is considered "bad."

Sexual morality is not a matter of blind prohibitions or taboos imposed on man from without; it is not the commandment of a God who wants to curb man's happiness. It is the acceptance of what it is to be human with all its exigencies. A "fault" is recognized when a particular way of acting makes it impossible for a person to grow in love. Sexual behavior which has such consequences must be rejected.

What has been said above indicates the appropriateness of early sexual education. The child must become aware of sexuality and its importance in the life of man, and see that there is no reason to make a taboo of it. He must, on the contrary, recognize it as a force which will later help him to grow in love.

As discussed in Chapter IV, an adolescent finds himself confronted by this new sexual force which is awakening within him. His sexuality introduces into his life a confusion out of which he must make some order if he is ever to discover his identity. This is the age at which sexual experience is highly related to the search for identity.

Masturbation is a phenomenon which is prevalent at this age. But, since it is an autoerotic experience, it does not generally help man to come out of his solitude, and so it cannot teach him really to love. The adolescent will have to move gradually from this autoeroticism to heteroeroticism. This is part of the whole process by which he will forget his "own little world" in order to transcend his solitude.

It is important to realize that masturbation is an effect of immaturity rather than a cause. It is more important to remedy the reasons for masturbation than to tackle the symptom itself. In adult life, masturbation is often a sign of regression. In the face of the difficulties of integrating himself in a given situation, the person returns to auto-eroticism. As with the adolescent, it is not by efforts of the will that he makes progress in eliminating the symptom; it is only insofar as a man succeeds in clarifying his roles, his function, and his relationships with himself and others that the symptom disappears almost by itself.

Another adolescent problem is that of discovering in what direction one's sexuality will develop. At this period a man is not yet completely polarized in his masculinity, nor a woman in her femininity. Since society often encourages contacts between persons of the same sex while simultaneously discouraging mixed relationships, it is easier to make friends with people of the same sex rather than with people of the opposite sex. This may even at times cause some adolescents to become homosexual. There can be psychological reasons which prevent a person from developing heterosexually, too. He may, for instance, be afraid of people of the opposite sex; in this case, the image of father and mother is very important. A man who has an extremely possessive mother, for example, may have great difficulty in loving another woman.

Homosexuality has always been rejected from the moral point of view. It would seem that the main reasons for this are both social and personal. From the social standpoint, homosexuality is undesirable because it does not lead to the procreation of children. In agrarian societies, where the presence of children constitutes a particular wealth, homosexuality is an economic threat. It is a type of relationship which is of little use to the society. In modern society, this social aspect is much less relevant.

At the psychological level, homosexuality is often a regression or a refusal to accept that the other can be really different. This may also be accompanied by a refusal of any generativity. Homosexuality can thus be a form of psychological illness. For reasons which we will not go into here, a homosexual may have difficulties in reaching the succeeding stages of the normal life–cycles. In certain milieus, homosexuality appears as a fad or a sort of liberation from taboos. Sometimes there is even organized proselytism in this direction. If this is the case, we are dealing with a social phenomenon rather than with a psychological regression. In any case, persons with homosexual tendencies can often use the advice of a psychiatrist in order to make progress toward more mature loving.

In the search to find a balance between intimacy and isolation, the young adult must come out of himself to meet the other. Gradually, he comes to know how to use his erotic drives in learning to love. But since this is not easy, and immature eroticism is liable to kill a new–born love, there may be a regressive return toward autoeroticism. Even if this danger is avoided, the task of learning how to love, of learning how to humanize one's eroticism remains.

Too often, especially in our commercialized society, sexuality is seen as a need to be satisfied. At the extreme, sex appears as an animal or inhuman satiation, and the important distinction between sexuality and genitality is lost. Sexuality must be appreciated as part of the very makeup of a human being while genitality refers to that which is directly concerned with the functioning of the sexual organs. The experience of one's own sexuality and genitality may seem baffling, troubling, and traumatic. For the sexual desire is shot through with ambiguity: it is both frightening and fascinating, terrifying and exciting, aggressive and receptive.

If one stops at the level of aggressiveness and fear, then all sexual relations will resemble rape. The other person becomes either the one posssessed by me or the aggressor threatening me, an intruder to be feared. Sex becomes a source of pleasure, but also something repugnant. It is not permeated with trust and acceptance of the other. The other is lusted after, even if he does not want to give himself. But sex is quite another thing if, through the body, the other person is sought and respected. Then sex is no longer aggression against the other and no longer provokes fear, but becomes mutual tenderness. An erotic gesture such as a caress becomes human if one knows that it is not aggression, and that it is accepted in trust by the other. Love is then no longer a conquest but a tender acknowledgment of the other. Tenderness is at the heart of the sexual act. In the words of Nietzsche: "In true love, it is the soul which envelopes the body." Tenderness, in the caress which expresses it is deeply human and respectful of the other.

As a human being learns to love tenderly he creates a truly human sexuality for himself. Genuine love in its physical expression tries to avoid everything aggressive in order to be genuinely trusting and tender. This is extremely important for morality. A love which is not true tenderness is not an expression of the law of love and charity even if the lovers are married. Learning to love, therefore, involves learning to dominate one's aggressiveness and suppress one's fear of the other. Asceticism is intrinsic to love.

All love is both communication among persons and the acceptance of differences which distinguish them. Love is limited communication, for there is no communication which can completely quench the thirst of man's heart. This finite quality of human communication implies the possibility of continual development. The sexual drive can become more and more humanized and an even deeper means of communication. If this growth does not take place, sexuality follows the psychological law of accustomization; it becomes routine. For love to survive, one must go beyond the equilibrium between love and work toward generativity in the thrust to transcend selfishness. This potential for growth is first encountered during the difficult period of adjustment before marriage where we face the problem of pre-marital sex.

A child should not be born if there is no family cell to welcome, love, and educate him. This is obviously a very important fact. Men are responsible for what they engender. As long as sexuality is seen solely as linked to reproduction, the problem is absolutely clear: before marriage, there can be no question of sexual relations. But, with the awareness that sexuality is also a human form of communication, there comes the realization that during the time of engagement, there is a growth in the tenderness which leads to the physical gift of self. Yet, there are still very good reasons from abstaining from pre-marital sexual relations both from a psychological viewpoint as well as a moral one.

Love is not simply a private affair; it is lived out within a society. When two people love each other, they want to commit themselves to each other, to learn to love together. This commitment, however, is to be public, for the love of two always exists within a world of others. Those who are in love will want, then, to express their commitment not only to each other but also to society. The physical gift of self really achieves its full dimension only with the setting up of a home. This is the basis for the institution of marriage.

Awareness of the surrounding society is already the first step toward the fruitfulness of love. After marriage, society accepts and promotes the couple's desire to be together and so creates the psycho-social security needed for the harmonious development of sexual communication. If this is lacking, there is a fear that the sexual relationship will be a source of anxiety for the couple, especially for the woman.

Moreover, delaying sexual relations until the commitment has been made public is a highly significant gesture. It is a declaration that this sexuality will be human. The relationship is put under the sign of love, and not under that of sexual need or of the need of a sex partner. The sublimation that this delay calls for can be for many people the source of a deepening of love. The refusal to wait may be an expression of the inability to control aggressiveness. If this is so, the relationship is liable to be lived in an atmosphere of rape rather than an atmosphere of love. This can engender a certain insecurity in the couple, with the added insecurity of the more or less secret nature of their relationship. If fear of sexuality is still present, this could be a serious problem for the future growth of love. From this viewpoint, waiting until marriage speaks a whole new language. It tells the loved one that there is nothing to fear and that the aggressiveness inherent to love is under control. Each partner then feels respected.

On the other hand, waiting until the time of the wedding can sometimes have unhealthy psychological and moral implications. Some couples wait until the wedding simply because they are afraid of sex. They see nothing human in it. After marriage, they accept it, but do not see it as human communication. In this case, waiting until marriage is liable to be a resignation or an abdication; in order to escape the task of integrating one's sexuality, fear is disguised as moral obligation. It is lying to oneself. But here, too, great prudence is called for. Fear is not overcome by moving ahead or by rushing in. If one or both partners has a fear of sex, that fear can only be overcome in the measure in which mutual respect and loving communication show that there is no cause for it.

Waiting until marriage for sexual intercourse seems to be a general principle for ideal situations, that is, situations in which psychology is evolving normally and in which the organization of society is such that commitment in marriage can take place at the moment when the dynamics of the couple's love brings them to that stage. Outside of ideal situations, it is necessary to study in detail what is the best way for the couple to grow in love. It is, however, essential to see the serious drawbacks of sharing sex when people do not fully share the rest of life. One of the signs of maturity in a couple will often be that they do not hesitate to consult an adult counselor who, without dictating to them what they should do, will help them to become truly aware of their possible options.

As we saw in the elaboration on the life-cycles, love normally develops into fruitfulness, whether spiritual or physical. Fruitfulness is an openness which, when it is physical, is expressed arithmetically as one plus one equals three. This is what prevents love from closing in on itself, from becoming selfish and bogged down in pseudo-intimacy. Couples who cannot have children might in some way express a spiritual fertility. Sometimes this can be done by adopting children; sometimes, by assuming a different kind of responsibility for other human beings. The human character of procreation is important; it is a question of persons and not of objects. A human being will not find fulfillment if he dedicates his life only to objects, projects, and institutions.

A serious problem arises when, for one reason or another, a family may have no more children. It may be a question of physical health, of economic necessity, psychological need, or other reasons. A couple who come to the conclusion that they cannot have children should examine carefully how their love will express its fruitfulness.

Related to this question of the fruitfulness of love is the question of faithfulness in love.

After the rather self–centered enthusiasm any encounter brings with it (whether it be falling in love or committing oneself to a cause), one is faced with one's responsibility to the other and to the situation one has created. Our deeds follow us; they change both reality and us. The unfolding of a commitment in time implies that man's growth to maturity goes on; an adult love is one which is capable of *fidelity*.

Promises are essential to existence; they are the acts by which a man declares his life projects, even if the realization will never exactly match the expectation. To be a man implies that at some times, in spite of ignorance of the future, one looks at his life and declares, "this is what I want to do with it." If a man waited for complete clarity before deciding and committing his future, he would never do anything. Nevertheless, a man's commitment is based on insight concerning who he is, what his surrounding situation is, his aspirations (both idealistic and realistic), as well as his awareness of the needs, the invitations and the calls of life itself. A promise or a commitment is a response to all of this, a step toward the future. When the commitment is public, it engenders a responsibility to society.

A commitment does not so much express an assurance as it expresses a hope and a will to realize something in spite of the crises inevitable in its realization. In a marriage, for instance, both partners express their commitment unconditionally to make their union and their love grow through all the difficulties and the crises which will inevitably arise. Because of the tensions of life, and the mistakes people make, there will always be a moment when the relationship becomes strained. The commitment declares that today, at the moment of the promise, one has decided to seek, during the time of the trial, a way to grow in love. By the promise one foresees the hour of difficulty and commits oneself to finding a solution for it. Thus does one forbid oneself the easy way out which would consist in abandoning the project at the moment of trial. Without this will to overcome difficulties, any love and any human project would soon come to an end.

A promise makes a man someone "you can count on" and

85

so is essential to life in society; without commitment it would become impossible to trust persons and life would be reduced to nearly total isolation. All of life in society is built on promises which make others reliable persons with whom one can work and establish solid relationships, despite the uncertainties of the future.

It is normal to encounter difficulties in realizing a commitment, for a human decision is not based primarily on an understanding of what is really going to happen, but rather on what we imagine the future will be. When we enter into a relationship or when we plan a project, there is always an imaginary projection of the person of the other or of the future situation. We often seek in the other what we lack, rather than the person himself; thus psychology has shown that every encounter involves some narcissistic seeking. It is the same for the choice of a profession, of a state in life, of a position. There is always a kind of "honeymoon" feeling. This feeling is good and should not be repressed; it supports the "visions" of people. But, growth of the individual implies that he goes beyond this in order to meet reality rather than to remain in the imaginary. Then the other becomes truly another and not "another me"; then a project does not remain simply a dream.

The process of growth implies two steps. In a first moment the identification of a person with what he desires is perceived as a kind of immersion. Often this first perception takes too little account of what is real and what is dream. The process of growth implies that identification with the other is done in full awareness of his "otherness"; the reality of his being is different from mine. A promise, by its openness to the future allows this growth and perception; it denounces the ambivalence of a narcissistic seeking in order to open the horizon onto an unknown otherness.

An example may clarify the effect of a promise. If a person intends to do something for another, but has not yet

86

committed himself, the project is fully his and he completely controls the situation. But when he decides and commits himself to do it, the situation has changed and he has a feeling of responsibility to himself and to others. He is now forced to distinguish reality from his dreams. A promise between persons is thus a bond of justice. The term "justice" designates a relationship in which the parties are aware that they are different and agree to share that difference. By "justice" a person gives another *rights* over his otherness. If a person commits himself to do something for another a new relationship has been built; such a person no longer has the right to consider his action only his own: it belongs also to the other. Loving other people has to begin with a recognition of their rights. Justice which recognizes that others are distinct from us and have their own rights is a presupposition of any true love relationship. In any other case love would be sheer intrusion.

A deep commitment to oneself and others is an essential part of a man's becoming an adult. As long as one is not capable of taking full responsibility for the statement, "this is what I am going to do with my life," one remains a nomad without roots. But by an explicit commitment, a man really takes his place in society. It is this insertion in society which determines the meaning of the virtue of fidelity; the foundation of fidelity is the *reality of persons* and not things, ideas, institutions, or projects. A commitment is not so much a statement that one will perform a certain deed as it is an affirmation that one assumes a responsibility before others: people are the reality to whom one commits oneself.[1] Although this commitment is ordinarily professed

1 It might be more exact to speak of a perpetual commitment only when it has revealed itself to be such in time. Before that, one can only say that the commitment is unconditional; one cannot, without presumption, say that it will be perpetual. There is even a way of feigning a perpetual commitment which hides something else: the desire of dominating or fixing a future which belongs only to God. In fact,

87

within a social institution such as marriage or celibacy, a man does not bind himself to certain actions, to a state, to a situation; he binds himself only to persons (God or others). The object of fidelity is not the *literal* content of a promise, but the *persons* toward whom one has made oneself responsible. It is possible that maturity is attained only at the moment when one commits oneself to *someone* and not just to ideas or projects.

A promise thus situates a human being within a set of relationships with persons who, by the very fact of this commitment, acquire certain rights in justice over him. This is the responsibility of husband and wife toward each other, of parents toward their children, of teachers toward their students, of public officials toward their constituency; of priests and religious toward their fellow Christians, etc. In all these cases, the result of the promise is the creation of a bond (generally incompletely defined), which it would be irresponsible to neglect.

There are, then, two essential elements of an adult's fidelity: a *promise,* which situates him within a responsible life project taking into account both his particular situation and his whole being, and the acceptance of the reality of the obligation which his actions (or chance, or the mistakes of others) have produced. In light of this, and as an example, we will briefly examine the meaning of the call to indissoluble marriage and of the crises met in the carrying out of commitments.

All too often, the vocation to indissoluble marriage is considered a trap in which married people are caught. Once married, there is no way out; they just have to manage. It is too bad if they are not too happy; "they must follow the path of duty." Such a notion of conjugal fidelity is essen-

---

in speaking of a perpetual commitment, one refers to the intention or desire of the one making it, rather than to factual reality.

tially false for it totally neglects the couple's growth in love and reduces something which should be dynamic into something fixed once for all. Indissolubility of marriage would be better understood as a *call* addressed to the spouses. When the marriage is in trouble, it seems better to suggest that they deepen their relationship to the point where they discover that they can grow—perhaps through forgiving acceptance.

A promise is a projection into the future; it sets the direction which a person determines to live. Since, however, a promise can only be expressed according to the light of the moment, it would be irresponsible to consider fidelity only with respect to the content of a promise. It is necessary to include the new elements brought about by change and its consequences. By the public exchange of marriage vows, the spouses commit themselves to each other and before society to the search for imaginative and positive solutions to the crises that they will meet. This promise can be an essential element in the crises that come for it implies that the couple understand that they must work together toward a positive solution. The promise anticipates the crisis without yet knowing its content. It does not, however, imply that a solution will always be found.

Fidelity is not a set thing; the actual fulfilling of a promise is always different from the way one imagined this fulfillment. To state that fidelity simply is the accomplishment of *what* was promised, is to neglect the necessity of adaptation, and faithfulness to reality. Every promise implies some imaginative creativity which goes far beyond its content. Although promises are not to be taken in an enslaving literalism they must be taken seriously. Without them life would quickly flounder in nomadism and love would become impossible. Which factors must then be taken into account when a promise seems impossible to keep?

In the case of crisis, there are two extremes which define

the limits of the problem. On the one hand, wounding or harming persons in the name of an abstract fidelity must be avoided. On the other, there is the possibility of irresponsibility in the name of freedom and fulfillment which is inadmissible in an adult. Consequently, imaginative and creative solutions must be found which allow the fulfillment of all involved. It is in that imaginative and creative attitude that true fidelity to the promise consists. Such a point of view is much more demanding than "literal" fidelity. Since the resolution of a crisis is never what one imagines, every crisis is a call to grow. It is essential, however, to point out that the fulfillment of the persons involved may sometimes come through renunciation for the sake of deeper love.

This is why, in moments of crisis, no one can judge his own situation. The final decision of course depends on the individual and as such must be respected. The response to a crisis, however, is liable to be unrealistic and narcissistic unless one confronts it before another who can help one see the full extent of the commitment which is challenged. Checking with others promotes fidelity by preventing the impulsive conclusion that the crisis is insoluble. It stimulates imaginative thinking and helps people discover unforseen solutions. It also avoids the fostering of a fidelity which is in fact blind obedience to the law or to the superego, rather than an overflow of love which flexibily adapts to reality. It may happen that a crisis is indeed insoluble and that the only growth possible is to live in breaking the commitment or perhaps even in accepting that one has failed.

The manner of expressing one's fidelity to a commitment can never be determined absolutely. Insofar as a commitment influences the future, it should be kept, and this is all that any law can reflect. But insofar as it is a matter of being faithful to the reality of *people,* the literal application of the commitment should give place to a deeper fidelity beyond the law. In the end, though, each one must make his own decision, realizing that he cannot know for certain whether the chosen solution is the best one or not.

When someone decides to break a promise, it is important to accept that fact as a part of reality. For the person himself, it is a matter of living with that decision, even though he is never absolutely certain it is the best one. It is not always easy to live with this uncertainty. That is why the refusal to anxiously go over the past is often a proof of maturity. To accept oneself and to believe one is accepted as the person one has chosen to be is also a mark of confidence in others and in God. But if one realizes that the choice has inflicted injury on others, reparation is imperative. Yet even in this case, sterile remorse would be useless. If a bad choice results in a situation it is impossible to get out of, fidelity to reality will then mean the actual living with that reality produced by the mistake.

Those who witness another person breaking a promise have no right to judge him. Even more, true love will accept the other's choice and, as far as possible, assume that the decision was made in a responsible way. No one has the right to take upon himself the mission of approving or disapproving another's choice. Jesus' words to the adulterous woman remind us of this: "Go neither do I condemn you; but sin no more." To refuse to judge does not imply that one considers behavior indifferent. It implies rather that breaking a commitment can manifest a deep fidelity to a reality as well as a refusal.

At the social and personal levels, breaking a commitment always poses a problem. Breaking a promise can be a sign of failure insofar as one was not able to make of the future what one wished. But this is no reason to condemn people. Condemnations are often psychological reactions compelled more by fear of the deviant behavior than moved by love. Often, without realizing it, the one who condemns another

91

expresses that he needs to judge in order to strengthen his fidelity to his own commitment. Severe judgment sometimes even covers a secret jealousy toward someone who does something one does not dare to do. To look lovingly upon a broken commitment implies at the same time both clear-sightedness about the reality of the failure and creative hope.

In conclusion, an essential note to human life is fidelity to reality and to people. Without commitment, existence would lose its meaning. Promises establish relationships of justice between people and help them to go beyond a narcissistic view of life. These promises should be taken seriously but fidelity to them cannot be turned into a negation of real love. Fidelity should never be geared to things or institutions, but to people; that is why faithfulnes to the reality of people can lead to departure from the literal content of a promise. Fidelity to reality and persons (including self) is characterized by an imaginative creativity through all the crises of life.

For Further Reading

Chirpaz, François, "Le Corps" in *Initiations Philosophiques* (Paris: Presses Universitaires Francaises, 1969).

A beautiful "phenomenology of the body."

Cooper, David, *Death of a Family* (New York: Pantheon Books, 1970).

An interesting description of the weaknesses of the modern family. The author, a psychiatrist, presents heterodox ideas on the subject. The book is instructive, although difficult totally to accept.

Marcel, Gabriel, *Le Monde Cassé* (Paris: Desclée de Brouwer, 1933).

A play which has forgiving encounter as the basis for its plot.

May, Rollo, *Love and Will* (New York: W. W. Norton & Co., 1969).

> An important contribution to psychology. The chapters on "Love and Death" and "Intentionality and Therapy" are especially recommended.

Oraison, Marc, *Being Together* (Garden City, N.Y.: Doubleday & Co., 1970).

> An excellent presentation of the topic of interpersonal relations. Communication and mutual respect are considered the basis for all such relationships.

Chapter VI

EDUCATION

One of the major concerns of the man who has reached adulthood is the formation of the next generation. Although this task of education poses a certain number of problems, the educator-educated relationship provides every human being with opportunity for growth.

Very often, teaching is presented merely as a way of transmitting knowledge. Although there is some truth in this concept, it is too limited. Teaching is much more than just the transmission of knowledge, the handing over of the word. For education to be successful, the word (teaching) of the educator must return to him renewed and changed by the student who has been able to make it his own. Teaching will thus imply a certain amount of tension resulting from the encounter of two generations. Children and adolescents educate adults as much as they are educated by adults.

One of the first aspects of education is the face–to–face encounter of the teacher and the student (or of the parent with their children). This confrontation may appear of little consequence but it is, in fact, deeply significant. The educator is usually older than his pupil. Consequently, he knows that the future does not belong to him but to the student who is there confronting him, and who is still unknown to him. The student, by the very fact that he belongs to the future generation, reminds the adult that sooner or later, he will have to face decline and death. But the new generation also represents a hope for the future which is still uncertain since youth is unsure what it will make of that future. This is why in the encounter of an "educator" and the "one to be educated" there lies the entire mystery of life and death with all the unknown forces it contains. In meeting the teacher the child has a foreboding that little by little he will be called upon to come to grips with a world where there will always be new people entering his life. As for the adult, he knows that in the child lies not only the future of society, but also the person who will take his place. He knows that this coming together of their lives will threaten his security and oblige him to face the conclusion of his own career.

The adult who does not experience some fear before the mystery of education can only be considered as unaware. At first sight, this anguish is diffuse and general, but if one examines it more closely it is made up of several elements: fear of losing acquired prestige, fear of losing the authority one possesses, fear of losing the privilege of being the one who educates. To become an educator means, perhaps, to accept the risk of losing all these things. It also means asking oneself anguishing questions: "What do I have to say? Do I really have anything to say? What are the repercussions of the words I use?" In this way youth obliges the adult to face the reality of his limited human condition. Mature educators accept this confrontation; many however become frightened and refuse it.

This refusal is expressed in two opposing attitudes. The adult, unyielding and set in his privileged position, can become paralyzed by fear and therefore lose all creativity. But he may also, in face of his inability to cope with the vitality of the young people, try to become "one of them" and, instead of leading them, only imitate them. In either case, he tries to escape the challenge implied in all education. But if the educator really accepts this challenge of confrontation, if he accepts his limitations and at the same time consents to give way to others (and to God), he undertakes with his students a process of mutual education. He knows that in one way or another, the young students will take him further than where he is today. Finally, he accepts the fact that an educator is not simply one who gives, but fundamentally the equal and the brother of the one whom he must educate; he will have to receive from him as well as give.

Having accepted such a confrontation, the educator now realizes that his mission goes far beyond the face-to-face meeting of two human beings. In the name of a whole society he has to transmit its cultural and scientific heritage to the young students. He can neither discount nor absolutize this heritage. He must transmit it as he understands it, aware that his own understanding is never complete. This transmission is not easy since the teacher must be careful not to make his word absolute and at the same time not to mutilate the message of the past.

Perhaps the most formative element in the relationship between teacher and student (or parents and children) is precisely this responsible and modest awareness of the educator's mission and of its limitations. The adult who succeeds in transmitting a message, which, though authentic is acknowledged as limited, teaches something about the human condition; he teaches how to be at ease with the insecurity of finiteness.

Having first accepted his own limitations, the educator can and must throw himself into the task of adapting the language of the past to present needs, and of creating new modes of expression for the values of the culture. But in this process of re–creating the message which is to be transmitted, the teacher and his students will quickly realize that there are several possible paths that can be taken. A master is never anything but *one* master among many. Lest he absolutize his expression of the message and thereby curtail it, the educator must always leave room for other masters.

An adult can have far-reaching influence over a young person. This influence however must not be an exclusive one or it will simply create puppets instead of fostering an increased liberty. To avoid this pedagogical fault there is only one solution: the teacher must be aware that the responsibility of education is a shared responsibility. Every young person in the process of formation should have contact with many adults. This will create the psychological space necessary for continued growth in liberty, and will help any teacher realize that he cannot attribute to himself the sole responsibility and burden of forming the student.

This acceptance of a plurality of educators is not accomplished without awakening a certain anguish in the teacher. He is afraid that his pupils will not do as he says. This anguish is experienced even more intensely when it is a matter of ideologies. Pluralism, however, is becoming more and more necessary in the formation of the young adult in today's world. It would certainly not be wise to leave a young adolescent confused in the face of too many options, when he has yet to achieve a personal synthesis. It is essential however to confront the young adult with the fact of ideological pluralism. This does not mean showing oneself indifferent to truth, but on the contrary, it means underscoring the relativity of any particular school of thought and the transcendence of truth itself. If he does not become aware of the plurality of ideas, it is possible that the student might perceive truth as something belonging to a particular group, sect, or culture. But when an educator places before the mind of the student different thoughts and options, he indicates that mature people do not proclaim their own truth but let it speak for itself. Jesus said what, ultimately, every man should say after him: "My word is not my own." It is through such an interchange, which goes far beyond an intellectual message, that education helps the student and the educator to grow in a love which transcends their respective limitations.

Finally, this pedagogical process attains its goal. The child becomes an adult and although his education is never complete, he has no further need of a pedagogue; the goal of formal education is its end. But there are differences and ambiguities in the way this goal is conceived. Some teachers feel that education ends when a person has become like them. They have then succeeded, they think, in re-creating themselves in another. The disadvantage of this way of thinking lies in the fact that if the disciple has become identical with his master he has not become himself with all that he has to offer.

In reality, a successful education is gauged by another criterion. It is at the moment when the pupil teaches something to the teacher, when by a reversal of roles equality of functions is established, that one can say that the education is complete and has attained its goal.

The educator who, until this time, was principally an authority figure (and even a "father image"), now becomes the equal and friend of the student. The process of information reaches its conclusion only at that moment. As long as the student or the child has not succeeded in becoming a friend of his teacher, or is still afraid to teach *him* something, he is not yet an adult. But when this does happen, he begins to realize the meaning of those words of the gospel which tell us that we have no master on this earth for we are all brothers.

For Further Reading

De Certeau, Michel, *L'Etranger* (Paris: Desclée de Brouwer, 1969)
> An extensive development of the theme of "encounter with the other."

Freire, Paulo, *Pedagogy for the Oppressed* (New York: Herder and Herder, 1970).
> An explanation of how education might escape the pattern of paternalistic educators and passively receptive students. Education is presented as a way of becoming critically aware or "conscientized."

Illich, Ivan, *De-Schooling Society* (New York: Harper & Row, 1971).
> A strong criticism of our present system of education.

Chapter VII

AUTHORITY AND COMMUNICATION WITHIN THE GROUP

Everyone must learn to live within certain groups: the family, the school, the work group, the community, the nation. These groups provide the individual with many opportunities for growth in love, but they also raise many questions. How is personal freedom compatible with the existence of authority? How can an individual retain his autonomy in a group while at the same time recognizing and respecting the right to personal freedom of the others? What role does a member play in group decision–making? It is in these areas that many ethical questions arise.

The way an individual relates to authority is extremely important for his growth in love. In fact we can observe that a good many personality disorders, together with the inability to love, find their roots in what might be called an "authority complex." People who have not learned to relate to authority have great difficulty in progressing in love. They project their poorly integrated authority figures into every life situation, and as a result, make life very difficult.

There seem to be two principal modes of expression for authority in society. The first is status authority, as found especially in agrarian societies, where authority resides in the father or leader or "chief," or even in a council such as in an oligarchy. There is also "functional" authority which is an aspect of modern society where authority resides in the chairman, in the majority vote, or in the group consensus.

In Roman society, the father of the family was the absolute head of the family; he was both a political and religious leader for his authority was of divine right and was all-encompassing. The authority of kings and emperors was of this type. It was based on a transcendent power which gives it realm over all things. Even in non–religious governments such as those of Hitler, Stalin, Mao Tse-Tung, we find a similar view of authority. In each case we find a common element: the person holding the authority has a very special social status independent of his function within the group (as coordinator or as executive). This kind of authority is extremely efficient in a society where there is little role–differentiation. Since in such societies, little specialized training is needed to exercise authority, the leader is distinguished from the other members of the group by the fact that he is endowed with a special social status. Pascal observes of the "great" of this world that, "having only imaginary ability they are obliged to take on sham qualities which strike the people's fancy . . . and so they gain respect for themselves. . . ."

In modern society where authority is usually based on competence, and safeguarded by its own effectiveness it is no longer necessary to protect authority by giving it a "special status." Authority is recognized for its functional value and its existence is justified only by the service which it renders society. Functional authority takes two principal forms: direction and coordination.

Directive authority decides for the group what is to be done and is extremely useful at times when the situation demand a quick solution. Such an authority acts primarily by orienting the efforts of the group in a certain direction. Such is the situation of the captain of a sinking ship. In this case a solution must be found and it is the duty of the captain to find it.

Coordinating authority tends to encourage as much initiative as possible and so obtain maximum participation by the members of the group. This kind of authority is better adapted for situations in which one has ample time for decision–making and is centered more on motivating the group rather than on commanding it. The group leader does not begin by telling the members what they should do, but instead helps them become aware of their desires and capabilities. The real authority resides more in the consensus and participation of the members of the group than in the person of the leader. The principal function of the leader is to assist the group in realizing its hopes and to enable the group to make decisions. He will also play a special role utilizing techniques to reduce conflicts which cannot be resolved otherwise in the time available.

Group members will express varying responses to authority. Sometimes an attitude of initiative will be called out; at other times it will be one of submission. Submission will be particularly useful when the demands of the situation render initiative inappropriate. (This will almost always be the case in static society, and even in modern society in times of emergency.) Initiative is desired, but in difficult situations there is no time to discuss solutions at length; then the "better" is the enemy of the "good." This is why, for instance, the army discourages initiative during wartime. The same situation holds in those societies where roles are poorly differentiated; everything has to be well–ordered and too much initiative will only produce problems. In all these situations, authority is often exercised like that of the *pater familias*. But when it is a matter of employing all the competencies within a group to solve long–term problems, initiative becomes extremely important. It can still have certain disadvantages however since aggressiveness and unresolved authority conflicts manifest themselves in the guise of initiative.

Adopting an adult attitude toward authority is never an easy matter. Authority is first experienced within a system of education in which the parents structure the life of the child and make certain demands upon him. The child lives in total dependence on his parents who hold authority over him; the parents represent security and omnipotence. But an evolution in obedience must take place so that the young adult can relate to those in authority as equals who are simply exercising a different function.

If he has not achieved this, as an adult he will often react negatively to an authority figure. In the end, if he has not come to consider his father as a kind of friend with whom he can establish a peer relationship, he is liable to project his repressed aggressivity onto every possible authority figure. An authority complex can be manifested either by a negative reaction to anyone who represents authority, or by a total submissiveness to authority figures. An individual with such unresolved conflicts is likely to be a problem to the groups to which he belongs. He will create an even greater problem if he happens to exercise a function of authority in the group. He will often reproduce the very attitudes he is rebelling against. He will either exercise authority in a tyrannical manner and so force others to fear it as he fears it; or he will go to the other extreme and refuse to accept the responsibilities of authority because he is still afraid of it himself. In either case he no longer fulfills the "role" entrusted to him and there is *in fact* no authority in the group. Both attitudes can have disastrous effects, especially in the field of education.

It is not always easy to discern if one has really solved the authority problem. There is a tendency to hide one's own problem by projecting it onto the authority. There are certain signs which indicate this. If a fear of constituted authority is present it is good to ask oneself why, or if there is a tendency toward constant negative criticism with no offer of positive alternatives, one should examine if he is really participating in the life of the group.

At times, every man will experience the remains of a latent authority problem. When confronted with it, the only real solution is to accept it by striving to calm the conflict it arouses and preserve one's equilibrium. This takes both patience and a sense of humor regarding oneself and others. Maturity stands out most clearly in the man who accepts authority as a function within a group, and sees those who exercise this function as potential friends.

The child begins his socialization by an encounter with adult authority, but in adult life, he must learn to cope with groups of equals. If he wishes to grow, he must learn to live in a group. This is one of the most difficult things to accomplish. Every increase in a man's ability to love is in some way the result of his acceptance of the demands of life with others. This may occur in family life, at work, in school, in any of the many situations where people live together. Living together is not something which is easily learned and it is only mastered after a long apprenticeship. There are two possible approaches a man can take toward life in a group: competition or participation.

Competition demands that each individual try to outdo the other. A man will strive to excel at what the group deems important so as to be considered the "best" and thus receive certain "awards," especially esteem. Competition can be extremely efficient, but it has unpleasant aspects. Competitors often have the feeling that they have "snatched success" from the hands of others. Competition also creates certain tensions within the group. At the worst, it will produce a disintegrated group in which each member takes all he can with no concern for the others.

Willingness to participate is based upon the belief that

personal success at the expense of the group is not success at all. The important thing is that each and every member of the group should receive all the benefits of life in common. Personal advantage is then abandoned in favor of a greater common good. "One for all and all for one" expresses well the attitude of participation. In such a group everything is shared with no fear of the others. If the group is a basic community (a family or a religious community), its members will tend to share what they have, what they are and what they feel—their joys, sorrows, fears, etc. In such groups, no one member is left with a problem as though it were his problem alone; one man's problem is everyone's problem. Yet the group has no desire to suppress the liberty of any of its members; each must assume his own responsibilities and his decisions will be respected. In less tightly knit groups (such as school friends), the relationship cannot go to such depth and extent. No one expects a member to give himself to the group completely nor is the group itself the center of life of its members.

Both in this type of group as well as in primary groups individual freedom must be safeguarded or there will develop a "tyranny of the group." Yet it is still desirable that in any group—no matter what type—the member should achieve the greatest possible depth of sharing. This will demand a real maturity from the members if they are to avoid the twin pitfalls of group tyranny and individualism. The risks are great, especially since individualists as well as tyrants do not always realize what they are doing. There will always be those who "manipulate" the group and it is not always easy to discern legitimate manipulations from those which are not.

Every member's attitude has an effect on the entire group, but we cannot always say whether it is positive or not. There is, for example, a kind of "emotional blackmail" by which certain members of a group are able to stifle expression or impede the decision-making process. Emotional blackmail often amounts to a person's making it clearly understood that if the group takes up a certain subject or pursues a certain course of action he will retaliate. This kind of emotional blackmail destroys the cohesion of the group and creates feelings of frustration which are sometimes quite serious. But it may also simply express an unconscious defense on the part of certain individuals who fear possible group tyranny.

We can say that manipulation is illegitimate when an individual member or a sub-group leads the group in a direction which it did not choose. This can happen without anyone's being aware of what is really taking place, and without the actual conflicts ever coming to light. There are however certain situations in which the reciprocal tyranny of members of a group may impede real communication to such an extent that respectful manipulatory maneuvers are almost a necessity. When this happens, it is a good idea to call on an expert in group communication.

We must not confuse manipulatory maneuvers with group techniques, however. Offering a drink to the members of the group in order to relax the atmosphere is a technique. But offering the group a drink in order to avoid examining a problem which should be examined is a manipulatory maneuver. The main difference between legitimate manipulation (group techniques) and unhealthy manipulation is that the latter conceals itself while the former explicitly reveals its objectives. As soon as a person becomes afraid, he is tempted to manipulate the group. It is wise for such to be honestly and gently faced. In this way communication becomes easier and more open and the fear of conflicts vanishes because everyone in the group realizes that honest confrontation can result in growth. On the other hand, pseudo-unanimity will also be avoided. If there is no agreement, that fact recognized and acknowledged can provide a deeper basis for unity. In this way very deep unity can be built little by little. It will be a unity in which each individual feels himself respected and loved as much for what separates him from the others as for what unites him to them. In divided groups, the difficulties accentuate divisions; in a united group, difficulties lead to greater unity even if disagreement still exists.

In an ideal group there are no purely individual problems. Even one person's difficulties and problems are experienced by all the members of the group. This does not mean that a member of the group who has made a mistake need not admit it, for in this way he assumes responsibility for his own actions. Nevertheless all the members of the group take upon themselves the problem resulting from the mistake of an individual member. Knowing that every difficulty will be assumed by all the members and that no one will remain in his solitude, gives the group great security. It acquires a remarkable boldness and a real potential for decision-making and effectiveness. But this demands real courage, for everyone is tempted to camouflage his deficiencies.

Some individuals cannot accept the challenge of life in a group and they try to avoid facing the limitations revealed to them by the group. This weakness is often disguised under the appearance of strength; a stubborn rigidity masks this inability to cope with new challenges. The resulting situation is at its worst when such a person is in a position of authority; he projects an image of a strong and courageous leader, while he is simply afraid and responding to fear.

If he succeeds in making people believe he is strong, another problem arises when he is asked to face challenges generally presented only to strong persons. As a result, he becomes even more threatened and inflexible. To help him and to solve the problems caused by his rigidity, people should understand that he is weak and that a non–threatening approach is needed. When such a person gets support and consequently grows stronger, he often becomes more able to handle his role.

Influenced by a false conception of the dignity of man, many people try to hide their weaknesses, thinking that this makes them stronger. They do not realize, on the contrary, that the really strong person is the one who is not afraid to admit his limitations. One reason why some people refuse to admit their failings is that the members of the group are not ready to accept the mistakes of others, to take them as their own, but tend rather to pass judgment on them. Sometimes they will punish the members of the group who do not meet their expectations, for instance by refusing them esteem. A tyranny can be established which, in the long run, might destroy a group. Such destructive situations demand the ability to engage in personal confrontation.

To confront someone does not mean bringing an accusation against him. It simply means coming face–to–face with issues and persons in order to see the real situation. Confrontation does not mean going to a person and telling him that he is doing wrong or has a problem. This would not be a confrontation but an accusation. In the face of such an attack, people will usually become defensive and refuse real dialogue. Such accusations may even be a kind of subterfuge. The accuser is hiding something from himself and another's behavior has made him aware of it. The accusation of someone else is the obverse of his own fear in face of the threatening behavior.

Actually, if the behavior of another seems bad or inappropriate to me, the only thing I can be sure of is that I have a problem with regard to his behavior. It is quite possible, in fact, that the other's actions are completely justified and should not be changed. True confrontation consists of going to the other and revealing that one is troubled. I ask the other to explain why he acts the way he does and, if possible, to say something which will calm my uneasiness. Seen in this way, confrontation is no longer an accusation. The other will often give a real explanation, sometimes discovering the good reasons he has for acting the way he does. Confrontation then allows one to discover the truth in a particular situation. It should be remarked that such an attitude never initiates a kind of competition which assumes, "if he is right then I am wrong," or vice–versa. On the contrary, there is an attitude of cooperation. The persons involved search together for what is best so that they can come to an agreement. One way to achieve this in a group is the method of "consensus."

"Consensus" is a method by which a group can decide on what course of action it will pursue. This method aims for the maximum participation by each member of the group. Everything is decided by unanimity. This does not imply that each person in the group is necessarily enthusiastic about a particular solution. It does mean however that each member accepts as his own the decision of the group. He consents to it in depth, and supports it sincerely.

The advantage of this method of decision–making is that it demands that all members of the group assume some responsibility and gives each one the feeling of having participated in the group's commitment. When it comes to action, a decision resulting from the unanimous consent of the group leads to much less conflict than a decision imposed by an external authority. Basically, "consensus" should be used for any important decision of a group, even though at times people will have to use techniques for resolving inevitable conflicts. In the democratic system the ideal is that when the group has voted on a decision (which is a conflict-reducing technique), all the members support the decision wholeheartedly. But in certain situations, it is possible to use the method of government by consensus at an even deeper level. This is the case in a family or in small groups. In these small groups, as far as possible, conflict-reducing techniques are rejected in order to try directly to obtain unanimity. There will be no recourse to a vote, a higher authority or adjournment before unanimity is reached. Unanimity will be required even to decide if a conflict-reducing technique will be required.

Arriving at unanimity implies a real ascesis. One must know how to question one's own desires each time it is necessary and how to liberate oneself from the egoism which makes us prefer our own solutions to any others. The conflict arising from disagreement must also be accepted and seen as a good thing in itself. One's own opinion must be defended while always remaining open to other possibilities. One must find the good in other points of view and try to harmonize with them. Such participation implies the courage to ask a question even if many in the group will not like it. It also implies the trust that each member is willing to let himself be challenged. Each person must, in one way or another, assume his responsibility in such a way that, once the decision has been taken, he can say that it is really *his* decision.

This also implies a refusal to maintain a "private domain." This does not mean that members of the group are refused the right to have a private life, but it is important that in a group working toward a decision there be no private domains, so far as the matter of the decision is concerned. If the group wants to create unanimity with maximum participation, everything must be brought before the group. If this has not been possible and something should touch what one member is "protecting," the unity of the group will be disrupted. Finally, there must be a refusal to judge one another and a complete acceptance of one another. This implies a very deep hope in the potential for growth of the others.

Throughout their task, the various members of the group

will be continuously called on to fulfill three principal kinds of roles: work roles, fellowship roles, and individual roles. Work roles have to do with the objectives of the group or with the mission to be accomplished. In fulfilling their work role, the members of the group facilitate and coordinate efforts toward the definition and solution of a particular problem. The work roles include: initiating new ideas; stimulating the group; asking for information and opinions; offering personal opinions and intimate convictions; explaining in what way one is not in accord with the objectives of the group; giving information as an expert or according to acquired experience; orienting the group and defining its position with respect to its goals; suggesting alternatives; summarizing or coordinating relationship among the ideas and suggestions of the group.

Fellowship roles are oriented toward the functioning of the group as a group. Their aim is to alter or maintain the work level of the group and to strengthen or redirect it cohesiveness. For example: facilitating the participation of others, encouraging them; giving one's agreement or support; showing affection and cordiality; expressing understanding and acceptance to others; setting forth an ideal for the group; observing the group process and pointing out what it has achieved; seeking ways toward compromises admitting one's personal mistakes; helping the others to feel at ease; participating in the activity or the decision of th group.

Individual roles are harder to define; they are directed toward the assertion of the needs of individuals in th group. They allow each one to express his feelings and t achieve his own personal goals. In many groups, the expression of individual needs is considered as something unfortunate. There are shades of meaning which must be considered at this point. If the "ideal group" is considered a one in which individual needs are so respected that the never have to be asserted then we must admit that this ideal is utopian, and even unhealthy. It is quite normal that an individual should be obliged to affirm his personal needs, to defend himself and protect himself against tyranny of certain members of the group. However, an ideal group member will avoid letting his individual needs limit his participation in his work and fellowship roles. Nothing is more difficult in a group than acquiring a true balance between a measure of egoism and a total participation.

Individual roles are often negative but they are sometimes the only way to make a group aware that there is a problem. Among such roles we can list: openly showing a lack of interest of nonchalance, cynicism or clowning; seeking to dominate the group of individuals; disparaging others; subjugating or manipulating the group; attacking the group or its members without reason; joking with aggressiveness; using emotional blackmail; seeking to concentrate attention on oneself; reintroducing, without valid reasons, problems already solved or bypassed; opposing whatever has been decided; asking for help or sympathy either out of insecurity or out of overestimation of self or— (and in this case the role would be positive), in order to show that it is important for the group to take each individual into account; using the group as an audience for one's own opinions, ideas, or feelings.

Even though most of these roles are very negative they are still important. Emphasis is to be put on the importance of realizing that there are personal needs within a group. It is a fellowship role of great importance to share one's fears, worries, and needs. Fulfilling such a role shows a very real trust in the other members of the group. A group in which the expression of individual needs is disapproved risks becoming, in the long run, quite unhealthy.

For Further Reading

Phillips, Gerald M. and Erickson, Eugene C., *Interpersonal Dynamics in the Small Group* (New York: Random House, 1970). As the title indicates, this is an in-depth study of communication within a group.

CHAPTER VIII

SOCIAL AND ECONOMIC LIFE

The principles of creative love and respect for the other have important applications even in the field of economics. Although material goods are often a divisive force in human relationships, material goods can create strong ties among men.

When a man sets out to carry a very large log, for example, he soon realizes that it is too heavy a load to carry alone. In asking someone for help, the log creates a bond between him and another. So too, economic relationships can be the point of departure for deeper human relationships, although it does not always happen that way. One of our present–day problems arises precisely from the fact that economic relationships are often limited to pure exchange. Besides exchange and trade, economy imposes working in factories, learning in colleges, etc. These are limitations of freedom. These limitations will always be there and should be included in economic calculations. Similarly gratuitous gifts will also be part of any economic system and should be part of the calculations also.

In our capitalist society the emphasis is given almost exclusively to the relationship of exchange and we become almost unconscious of the constraints inherent in the system itself. Actually, if the economy is to run properly, all the norms prescribed by the "organization" must be accepted, and as a consequence controls and constraints characterize our capitalist system. In the socialist system, on the other hand, there is a tendency to consider programming as a substitute for constraint and control. In both systems we have lost sight of the place of gifts in life, and overlook the fact there are things which can neither be sold nor restricted; things like friendship, a smile, kindness. It is important that we reintegrate all these values into our economic and social life.

All too often, too, progress is identified with material abundance. Nothing is more questionable. If it is true that abundance can lead to progress in human life, it can just as well engender alienation. The tendency of an affluent society to make persons simply consumer–producers is one of the deepest problems of our age. There is a tendency to subject the social and personal aspects of life to the economic aspect and in this way society becomes modeled according to the demands of the economy rather than according to human relationships and concerns. Restriction slips into the free enterprise system so subtly that it is never considered a part of the system. The very notion "social" is often reduced to an "enlightened" paternalism on the part of the economic organization. If we identify progress with economic production, what was once only a means becomes an end in itself. It is urgent for us realize that economy should be at the service of society, that is, at the service of human relationships, and not the other way around.

This change of outlook might imply a revision of the objectives of economics in order to form a *generalized economy*.[1] In this perspective, the social sciences would join together in order to define what human progress should be if it had as its goal the promotion of all the dimensions of man. Such a vision of economy might be outlined in the following manner: First, the objectives of the economy

---

1 Francois Perroux *Economie et Société*, Collection "Initiation Philosophique" (Paris: PUF, 1960).

would be to help man to accomplish what he wants rather than to increase his material affluence. Second, it would take into account the necessity of harmonious growth by integrating the crises due to change. Third, such an economy would be an economy of progress understood as the liberation of man from his alienation and lack of equilibrium. It would identify the various inequalities among men in order to correct them. Fourth, it would go beyond the distinction between the social and the economic; the economy would be returned to the service of society. Fifth, the economy would go beyond the interests of a single group to become planetary and open itself to all men.

Such a program forces us to realize that the present economic systems are still very inadequate. We seem more concerned with exploiting others than with promoting justice.

Exploitation is a notion which is very difficult to define because of the existence of what economics calls "rents." In the language of economy the term "rent" refers to profit or return derived from any differential advantage in production. It is a profit which does not arise from any kind of work but only because of the association of people or the discovery of wealth. These earnings would not exist if these people did not combine forces.

As an example of the existence of "rents" let us cite the difference in price between a car bought directly from the owner and one bought through a dealer. A personal agreement between the buyer and the seller dispenses with the "services" of the dealer and the difference of price arises simply from the association of the two persons; it is called a "rent." Should the money so saved go to the buyer or to the seller?

Similarly the association of developed and underdeveloped countries creates a tremendous "rent." Where does it go? And where should it go? For example, should the "rents" produced by the association of developed countries and

117

underdeveloped countries remain in the poor countries? Or is it legitimate for the richer countries to collect? It is difficult to determine.

One thing, however, seems certain. Exploitation exists when the relationship between two unequal parties is such that the inequality perdures. A relationship which would perpetuate inequality, especially for more than one generation certainly becomes unjust exploitation. Undoubtedly this is the type of relationship between developed countries and the "third world." Even the so–called foreign aid programs are often subtle means of maintaining an exploitative relationship in which the wealthy nation benefits at the expense of the poor nation. While there is no question here of declared violence and bloodshed, yet it really is unjust oppression. How is such oppression to be overcome—peacefully or through violent revolution? In order to destroy an oppressive system can we use methods which will do harm to certain individuals? Is it legitimate to permit violent revolutions?

To speak of violence in general is unrealistic. It is preferable to consider various types of violence. Which is more "violent," an oppressive society which crushes a segment of the population, or the responding revolutionary forces which attempt to bring about a drastic change? The external violence of revolt may sometimes be much less violent than the crushing weight of an unjust system. Yet the near-impossibility of knowing if the situation will be improved after the revolution must be seriously considered by the revolutionary. In the absence of such knowledge, it is difficult to determine a completely acceptable solution to social injustices.

There is no ready–made solution to these problems. The truth of the old adage that "the rich get richer and the poor get poorer" is hard to escape; but it is not at all obvious how this situation can be changed. It is a fact, for instance, that industries make twice as much profit when they trade with underdeveloped countries as when they deal with richer ones. The very aid we would try to give seems to trap us in an unjust system. Such a system has to be challenged. But how? On one hand, if power is confronted with power, violence will always be present; on the other hand, if oppression is condoned, an unjust society will continue.

Such problems cannot be solved only by individual decisions and good will. The system actually forces the person who wishes to survive to become an unjust exploiter. The man who does not pursue this path is liable simply to go bankrupt and be replaced by someone who is perhaps even more unjust. These problems will only be solved by changing the entire economic system—a real cultural revolution is needed. If such a revolution is welcomed with good will we can then hope that it will be a peaceful revolution; if it is not, this can be expected to be violent and totally irrational. In view of these questions, it is obvious that an individualistic framework of ethics is obsolete. If the situation is to be improved, there will have to be changes which go far beyond the actions of a single individual.

Up to this point we have posed moral problems primarily in terms of the personal choice of an individual wondering how he might best grow in love. We see now that this individualistic framework for moral or ethical reflection must be expanded to include social responsibility. As this chapter illustrates, morality is no longer limited to a purely individual question in a clearly defined setting; it faces much broader questions on a much larger scale. The following chapter will further explore this need for a social ethic, in uncovering the problem of an ethics of science. Further questions, such as war and peace, pollution, the relationship between rich and poor nations, cannot be developed in a book of this scope. The problem of the ethics of science, though not more important than the others, has been chosen to illustrate questions which arise when we go beyond an individual ethic to a social ethic.

For Further Reading

Berrigan, Daniel, *No Bars to Manhood* (New York: Bantam Books, 1971).
> An interesting book by someone who committed his life to the liberation of people in an unjust society. The chapter "Exit the King" and the section on Bonhoeffer's thought are particularly stimulating.

Kirkham, James F. *et al, Assassination and Political Violence: A Staff Report to the Violence Commission* (New York: Bantam Books, 1970).
> A detailed presentation of the data on a very hot question.

Lipset, Seymour M. and Solari, Aldo, eds., *Elites in Latin America* (New York: Oxford University Press, 1967).
> A treatment of the social problems of Latin America.

Perroux, F., *Economie et Société* (Paris: Presses Universitaires Francaises, 1959).
> A development of many of the ideas presented in this chapter.

Shoot-Out in Cleveland (New York: Bantam Books, 1969).
> The findings of the controversial commission which instigated a new awareness of the extent of violence in the United States. A basic document on the causes and meaning of violence.

Smith, Elwyn, ed., *What the Religious Revolutionaries Are Saying* (Philadelphia: Fortress Press, 1971).
> A series of essays by several revolutionaries who have found their inspiration in religious conviction.

Theobald, Robert, *Alternative Future for America Two* (Chicago: Swallow Press, 1970).
> An interesting book presenting possible alternatives for the society of the future.

Ward, Barbara, *The Lopsided World* (New York: W. W. Norton & Co., 1968).

What is our Western world doing to the underdeveloped nations? This is a fascinating attempt to answer that question. It will appeal especially to those who are sensitive to the morality of economics.

Wasserstrom, Richard, *War and Morality* (Belmont, Cal.: Wadsworth Publishing Co., 1970).

A treatment of war as a moral issue and its impications for our society.

CHAPTER IX

A NEW FRONTIER:
THE ETHICS OF SCIENCE

Within the perspective that morality cannot be confined to purely individualistic questions an attempt will be made to determine a few guidelines for an "ethics of science." Specific problems such as: "Are heart transplants ethical?" will not be considered so much as the more general problems posed by the increasing importance of scientific study in contemporary society.

Some of the questions which must be faced concern the responsibility of the scientist, the definition of his profession, the scientific community's growing awareness of itelf, the ambiguities inherent in scientific research, the true and false tensions between science and social action.

The scientific community about which we are speaking is not limited to university scientists who enjoy a relatively greater freedom of action than their peers employed in industry or applied developmental research. There are important differences between the two groups but they will not be considered here. Indeed, it will be assumed that the distinctions between pure scientists and applied scientists as well as between basic research and applied research are not useful for the point of view proposed here.

The ethics of science is virgin territory. Publications on the subject are scarce. In fact, until very recently, science hardly had any social repercussions but was rather the "hobby" of a few individuals. Today it has become one of the prime molders of our civilization.

Science gives man such power that he becomes master of his own progress and even of his own survival. Fifty years ago, no one could have worried whether humanity would destroy itself; man simply did not have the power. Today, however, it is quite possible for men to destroy themselves and so it becomes essential to creatively take the future in hand. This in turn changes man's relationship to his own existence. This evolution can be compared to the evolution of transportation. In the time of the ox cart, no one needed a steering wheel; on a race car, however, a steering wheel is critical. In the same way, the former rhythm of life permitted man to let things develop on their own while he waited for the outcome. Given the present acceleration of the development of science, however, if man does not master it, he will perish as its victim.

Simple statistical laws predict that if man leaves things to random choice, catastrophe is inevitable. If we leave the future simply to chance the risks become greater and greater and the very survival of man is threatened. Let us look at the ox cart and the race car again. If you go off the road a bit in an ox cart, you can get back on without great difficulty; but with a racing car, it would be almost impossible. This situation is critical and shows how high the stakes are in the scientific community's becoming aware of its responsibility.

When we speak of the need for men of science to "assume their responsibility," it sometimes conjures a picture of a kind of tribunal where men of science would be judged for what use they have made of nuclear energy, human genetics, the environment, etc. Their responsibility is set within a context of guilt and condemnation.

We do not here use the term responsibility in that context, but rather in the sense of the term "responsible parenthood." If a couple brings a child into the world, they are responsible for him. That does not mean that the parents are guilty of the mistakes which the child may make once he is an adult, but certainly they are responsible for the kind of education the child receives until he becomes an adult. Perhaps the responsibility of scientists, or more precisely of the scientific community toward humanity should be defined in the same way: the responsibility for bringing their own projects to full development.

It is the mission of scientists to see to it that their activities and discoveries help mankind. Consequently, it is for them to take into account the effect of a discovery when it appears in the field of scientific research or technology. Scientists are responsible for appraising the results of research when they are still in the area of theoretical science in order to become aware of the future implications. It cannot always be foreseen how new inventions or techniques will evolve after that, and it is absurd for example, to claim that Einstein is responsible for the atomic bomb which was built thirty-five years after the discovery of the Principle of Relativity. Yet, certain biologists (and indeed the community of biologists) may right now hold the responsibility for what will be the outcome of new discoveries in human genetics. They should be careful to transmit, along with new possibilities of their science, all the information necessary for humanity to use in the best possible way in order to protect itself against any possible abuses.

It is even more essential for responsible scientists to realize that they do not transmit only the *content* of their field. The scientific *method* and the scientific *vision* profoundly modify the surrounding society and culture.

As Marshall McLuhan, has shown in the bestseller, *Understanding Media,* what has changed our civilization is not new discoveries themselves, but the spirit of these discoveries, the scientific spirit. By envisaging a world in which science will allow us to *foresee* more and more, the scientific community builds up a *new type of relationship between man and his environment.* He is less and less likely to accept it as he finds it; he now fashions it. In doing this, science modifies the relation between tasks and play, passivity and activity, work and leisure.

At this level, it is false to say (as is often done), that inventions are morally "neutral" since it is only the use humanity makes of them which poses any ethical problem. By the sheer fact of their existence, such inventions transform the human environment. Scientific activity independent of its content, already presents an ethical question.

The scientific community should act in a responsible manner and this is the task of the entire community and not of isolated individuals, for science is not practiced in isolated individuals, for science is not practiced in isolation. The image of the solitary professor is outdated—research, discovery and responsibility are now group endeavors. A scientific ethics must treat of responsibility as a task which is incumbent upon the community of those engaged in the use of available data. This is probably the reason why the concept of scientific ethics is so misunderstood; the scientific community is only now beginning to become aware of itself. It is essential to understand this phenomenon.

Certain sociological sub–groups like the business community, the military, and blue–collar workers have become aware of their own existence and power as groups. These communities realize that they can influence the manner in which society evolves. Consequently, they hold real power and become necessary factors in any viable solution of specific problems which society faces. If, for example, big business is opposed to certain political alternatives, it has the means (whether we like it or not), to force the entire society to revise its objectives.

In some countries the military has just about the same

power. When these pressure groups unite, society is threatened with "one-dimensionality": a single group decides what may or may not be done. If, on the contrary, each community accepts the responsibility of consciously acting according to its own particular character, there is hope for a multidimensional society.

The scientific community has not yet completely realized that it can be an important element in any such coalition. Yet, in the modern world, if it refuses its special contribution, it can block any real progress. Like the business and military communities, it has real veto power, but it does not yet know this. Otherwise, it could add a new dimension to many debates, for it is preciely one of the few communities today capable of carrying weight with big business and the military. But in order to do this a responsible and aware scientific community is necessary. Such is not yet the case for the university researchers and even less for the scientists employed and controlled by industry.

The business community holds responsibility because it has become aware of what it is and how great is its influence. The scientific community is moving slowly toward this. Just as during the last century the working class became aware of itself, scientists today realize that they are necessary to the progress of society and responsible for their potential contributions. This is a new situation. To understand it, the historical context must be considered, and one must discern why the scientists have not realized their power until now.

The delay is probably due to the fact that the scientific community still refers to a self–image which goes back to the Middle Ages or the renaissance: the isolated scientist and a "disinterested" science. This image became outdated after 1850 when technological and scientific progress began to keep pace with one another. But it is still clung to and has become an obstacle to the scientific community's awakening to self–awareness. It leads scientists to abdicate their power of decision to university or industrial administrators.

The emerging image is more adequate. It sees the world of science as a community which is responsible for its own destiny and for its contribution to society. In the United States especially, after the "Manhattan Project," which developed the atom bomb, and the rude awakening of Hiroshima, scientists have felt more obliged to participate in public affairs. The transformation is not being made without difficulty, however, and many still resist, often in the name of disinterested science.

More deeply perhaps, there is a feeling of powerlessness and of inability. Scientists are only rarely prepared to assume responsibilities which imply a conscious commitment to the elaboration of culture and the future of society. With no training in community action or in techniques to combat modern bureaucracy, many prefer simply to surrender their social potential. Their ideal could be summed up as follows: "Leave us to our work; just give us what we need for our research and we will be quite happy." Accustomed to well–organized experiments in laboratories, rather than to political battles and discussions in committee, some scientists reject the latter. As often happens, lack of training leads to ineffectiveness in action and this, in turn, leads to a refusal not only to accept but even to admit their responsibilities. In order to form a responsible community, scientists must become conscious of the way a group acts, of how a community learns to work as a team, of how to handle the tensions of group life. The social formation of scientists is a whole domain which is still neglected.

The difficulty in changing should not be a case for surprise; it is a question of forming a new image of the scientist.

A profession can be lived passively or actively, as a nomad or as a pioneer. In the former case, the history of ideas together with mere chance construct a cultural pattern which defines the profession. This is the organization of a certain number of roles into a particular function in society. It usually implies that society demands a certain knowledge and certain capacities in the members of this profession while tolerating certain deficiencies and ignorances. The organization of a profession is not something done once and for all, but is affected by cultural evolution. The members of a profession who enter it cultivate certain behavior patterns so as to correspond to the ideal type (scientists, doctor, politician, etc.) projected by the culture. At the same time, their profession excuses them from certain tasks; a scientist, for instance, will not feel obliged to know political economy nor a politician to know physics.

But the concept of a profession does not remain static; it is continually defined by its members and by society itself. Those who live it actively do not organize their roles strictly according to the pattern of the past, but also according to the function they intend to exercise in the future. In this sense a professional community can redefine what it is. To an increasing extent doctors now feel obliged to have some knowledge of psychology as well as physiology. This being the case, they can redefine the domains in which they can be expected and demanded to be competent.

It is to be hoped that through the development of the responsible scientific community a new definition of the scientific profession will be elaborated. Today it is still determined by what its own prehistory has made of it. Scientific progress has changed the society around it and has modified the situation of science in relation to culture as a whole. It is about time to adapt our cultural and mental models of scientists to match these changes. For instance, we would consider "irresponsible" a company executive who knew nothing of "management," "public relations," "group dynamics," or "political economy." Is it normal, then, that we accept a scientist with no political, economic or administrative competence and even with no formation in the policies of science? Our culture still seems to consider and accept scientists as socially irresponsible beings, as if they were not among the principal purveyors of ideas, of culture, of intellectual and technological planning. Little by little, however, this situation is being modified. The responsibility of the scientific community has already been exercised in different domains during the last few decades.

The atomic bomb was constructed as a result of fear, fear that scientists had of seeing the weapon in the hands of Nazi Germany. Whatever one may think of Hiroshima, the Manhattan Project was an effort in responsibility. The feeling of responsibility within the scientific community is stimulated today by publications such as the "Bulletin of Atomic Scientists," which distributes the information necessary for the social formation of the scientist. An effort is being made to transform the deep tensions between ideological blocs into an almost sporting kind of rivalry for the conquest of the moon. Finally, the present cut-back of funds for scientific research in the United States is provoking a reaction among scientists which, however self–seeking it may be, obliges them to think together as a community.

For scientists, responsibility demands first of all the recognition of the ambiguities inherent in scientific research. We will discuss these ambiguities at two levels: that of the process of research and then of its content.

The very existence of the process of research and of technology, as previously stated, changes the situation of man *vis-à-vis* his environment. Now that he can transform and modify it in large measure, he is no longer the same person. Thus little by little the scientific mentality creates a new culture. To scientists falls the responsibility of participating to the best of their ability in the cultural changes which they provoke when they create a mentality in which primacy is given to the predictable.

At the content level, the ambiguity is twofold: one aspect is well–known, the other is not. What is well–known is that every scientific discovery contains a potential for application and that this potential can be utilized for better or worse. Everyone knows that atomic energy can be used to make atomic bombs or nuclear reactors. But the other side of the ambiguity is just as important: all scientific research and every scientific discovery is ambiguous because the scientific know-how used to obtain it could have been employed in discovering something else perhaps even more important.

Research whether basic or applied is a technical under-taking which requires an investment; if directed towards one area this is usually done at the expense of another. Every scientific discovery is ambiguous for it may hide the possibility of an alternate discovery which is a more valu-able and technically more feasible one. The invention of a new kind of camera, for example, may be very useful; but the discovery of a new food for developing countries might have taken place if one had employed an equivalent effort in that direction.

Without going so far as to believe that a gain in one field is a loss in another it must still be admitted that every scien-tific conquest raises a basic question: "What might have been achieved instead of this?" To study this question in depth let us consider the most contemporary example—that of the conquest of the moon. Man has walked on the moon. What might have been accomplished in its place? What might the same investments in another direction have pro-duced? Obviously we do not know. But that is precisely the problem. It would be reasonable to look forward to the adoption of the best scientific strategy possible. Otherwise, we are liable to realize that we are going nowhere. All mili-tary victories are not good; certain partial victories may cost the war. Perhaps certain scientific discoveries are simi-lar. Walking on the moon is an exploit and a victory, but what did it cost humanity? What could have been done in its place? It is not a matter here of our indulging ourselves in sentimental consideration on the subject, but of proceeding to a cold economic calculation. Is the effort invested in the space program well–placed, or is humanity going to find itself in the position of the man who buys a ticket to the theater but cannot enjoy it because his stomach is empty?

We should note here that it is not a question of sacrificing research for humanitarian reasons (we shall return to this question later), but of carefully choosing the object of that research. Research is no longer (or should no longer be), a group of boy scouts undertaking a new venture; scientific research demands both strategy and careful planning. Whatever blocks the possibility of further progress and intelligent research should be tackled first. But to get to this point, the scientific world must first extricate itself from individualistic patterns, for all too often a project is undertaken without sufficient reference to social values and goals.

There is also the parasite situation where scientific research enslaves itself to the caprices of different administrations and the possibility of being caught up in the vicious circle of "the budget." Due to scientific results, subsidies are given and, due to these subsidies, assistants and equipment can be acquired which will produce innovative and better results. All of this engenders a certain irresponsibility, for it never raises the basic question of the remote goals of research. In the end, scientists avoid the issue by stating that no one should question the disinterestedness of science.

To take a closer look at these two challenges to science, two questions must be asked: "Must we choose between scientific research and social action?" "Is there such a thing as "distinterested science?"

If the average man on the street is asked whether we should go to the moon, the answer is often couched in terms of a dilemma. "Either we use our resources and talent to go to the moon and benefit science, or we use them to feed the world and benefit mankind." The dilemma is always seen as a choice between the advance of science or the development of human life. Of course some say: "We can't give up scientific research; it is good for man to investigate the universe. We must go to the moon." But others retort: "We can't sacrifice the good of humanity to science. We should give up going to the moon in order to find a solution to problems such as world hunger."

We must not allow ourselves to be trapped in this dilemma because the choice is not between the advance of science or the good of humanity, but between two projects which are simultaneously scientific and human. Going to the moon implies scientific accomplishments and enormous techniques, but feeding the world implies the same accomplishments and techniques. These are two possible tasks for man and both very difficult. Going to the moon and feeding humanity are two very arduous technical feats. A few years ago both seemed absolutely impossible. Man decided to tackle one of these tasks and agreed to employ the necessary material and human resources. As a result he succeeded; man has walked on the moon.

But aside from this concrete result the moon project also produced a number of by–products. All the sciences, from electronics to physiology, benefited from a project undertaken in the name of astronautics. Can such results justify the undertaking? It would seem so, especially when we compare these developments with the meager progress in other fields for which funds are not allocated. But perhaps these projects which have not had such public support would also have produced developments as unexpected as were the by-products of the moon conquest. The conquest of the moon, for example, permitted very important discoveries in electronics miniaturization. Mankind now enjoys a level of worldwide communications which a few decades ago would have been unimaginable and which has had repercussions even in international relations.

At the moment we cannot "imagine" what would have been the by–products of a project undertaken to solve the problem of world hunger. This is a technical task as gigantic as any in astronautics and we have no idea what it would produce if we really set ourselves to it. This shows that it is not a question, on the one hand, of undertaking a scientific project (going to the moon), and on the other, undertaking a humanistic project (feeding hungry humanity). We are confronted with two technical problems, both extremely difficult. The world is aware of the possibilities of one because it has succeeded; those of the other are still unknown because it has not been undertaken with the same determination. But both are scientific projects of far-reaching significance.

It is false, then, to say that science would be sacrificed to humanism if we tried to feed the world. The latter is a technical project which would demand as much scientific research and which would produce as much technical progress as did the conquest of the moon. It is obvious that other sciences would profit in this case also. If we set ourselves to the task of feeding the world, it would be of immense profit, for instance, to biochemistry, sociology, etc. in the same way as the development of astronautics has produced advances in physics. In either case the advancement of science is assured. Results seem to depend more on the amount of the investment and the seriousness of the research than on the nature of the project undertaken.

If we accept this hypothesis, the question which then confronts us is: "Which is technology's top–priority project for today?" or, "Which project will open the horizon onto further advances?" We are concerned now with what might be called the "strategy of science"; in other words, what priorities are to be respected?

Unfortunately, the concept of scientific strategy is practically unknown. Nonetheless, scientific research can be compared to a military offensive. Armies do not just keep moving straight ahead, but they move in view of certain strategic objectives. Likewise within each particular scientific field, objectives are often very well–defined during colloquia and congresses. But when it comes to a question of interdisciplinary collaboration, individualism still rules.

It often happens that when a decision is not taken through conscious reflection it is dictated by factors of which we are not consciously aware. Perhaps the priority given to the conquest of space is nothing but the natural outcome of the forces which have shaped Western culture. When the possibility of conquering space opened up to us, we immediately jumped at the opportunity with almost no further thought. Our cultural past had already decided for us. For centuries, the Western world had dreamed of reaching the stars—the ultimate frontier, the symbol of all that was unchangeable and eternal. We had never directed our hopes toward a society in which man would have enough food to eat. Our dream of conquering space has come true, but has humanity been made any nobler by this choice or by this absence of choice?

At a time when technology has opened up unlimited possibilities to man, it might well be asked whether there is an absence of a certain creative energy or imagination. Is humanity really equal to the task of choosing its destiny? A person whose actions are determined only by his past experiences without being able to imagine new alternatives for the future is usually considered as stunted or infantile. Must we say the same of a society which is unable to determine its own future? There is no doubt that this is our present level of maturity. We inherit situations which are the result of cultural and historical factors, rather than definite decision and planning. It is necessary to take inventory of the

135

economic and human resources already invested in existing scientific projects. Then we must decide what we want to do with these in the future. Scientific progress must no longer be decided simply by centuries-old dreams or the commitments of the past.

It must be emphasized, however, that this is not a matter of deciding general criteria for establishing priorities. Unlike the problems in textbooks, there is no teacher's manual with answers to the problems. We will never know whether the solutions are better than the other alternatives considered or, even more, whether they are better than the alternatives considered or, even more, whether they are better than the alternatives we never thought of. Consequently, we must look for good methods of choice making rather than criteria establishing the content of good choices.

It is not our task here to recall what has already been said on the subject of communication and group dynamics. The social sciences indicate that the "best" choices seem to be the result of a consensus composed of people who contribute useful information assuring maximum participation of all. This consensus might be defined as a compromise to which the well–intentioned participants in the group can give their unreserved allegiance after all the data has been considered. It would thus be desirable that at every level of technological decision–making, the scientists involved be given all the data and be encouraged to participate in the decision-making process. The importance of collaboration among specialists of different but related sciences must be emphasized. The different points of view can liberate the group from the bonds of routine and hardened categories. Following the same principles, the scientific commissions which establish general objectives and accepted priorities should as much as possible be composed of representatives from all schools of thought, both social and professional, in order that a true consensus might be achieved.

Some object that science must maintain its "neutral position," that it must be "disinterested" in order not to be partner to the crass manipulations of business administration and to be faithful to its own principles without considering outside factors. But must not science follow the principle of effectiveness rather than disinterestedness? As E. Mach[1] showed nearly a century ago, it is probable that the essence of scientific progress consists in the development of concepts by means of which it is possible to describe physical reality in as precise a manner as possible and so be able to transform it. This implies that science, of its very nature, wants to be effective. It wants to foresee what is going to happen. Even more, by choosing this goal, it tends to eliminate that part of reality which is not measurable or cannot be defined in exact terms. Almost by definition, science concerns itself only with what is foreseeable; its interest lies in determination.

If this view of science is correct, then it becomes rather difficult to speak of "disinterested" science. On the contrary, science is interested directly and uniquely in the foreseeable and is part of an even vaster project of mankind—man's desire to feel "at home" in the universe.

It is important, of course, that scientists do not go astray in seeking short–range effectiveness. But once the long–range view of the situation is taken it is essential that the scientific project try to be as effective as possible. Nevertheless, even where science is practiced under the rules of "foresight" and "effectiveness," it includes another dimension which cannot be neglected. Science is also "an enjoyment," "a delight," a field where the process is as rewarding as the result—like the building of a cathedral. This expresses the contemplative dimension of science. The spon-

---

1 A celebrated physicist of the nineteenth century ("the sound barrier"). His treatise "An Historical and Critical Survey of Mechanics" has had an important influence in the field of physics.

taneity of scientific research cannot be eliminated under the pretext of effectiveness. When a human being tries to be too intense he loses his inner dynamism. It is always difficult to balance effectiveness and spontaneity, but, if science entirely eliminates "science for fun," it shuts itself up in a regrettable one-dimensional world.

In conclusion, science must decide what is its contribution to the elaboration of culture, live with this responsibly and re-define the social role and the "craft" of the scientist. It is urgent that more consideration be given to the ambiguities inherent in scientific research, not in order to abdicate the mission of science but to integrate it within the whole of human development. The scientist must become aware that he is fashioning a future society, whether by the models he furnishes for its thought or by the inventions and the new ideas he proposes. This implies that the whole of society must establish techniques for planning and decision making in order to determine (without hampering spontaneity), which direction scientific research should take. Without this awareness it is to be feared that the "brave new world" which Huxley described a few decades ago may soon become a reality.

For Further Reading

Civilization and Science, CIBA Foundation Symposium (New York: Elsevier, 1972).
  The reports of a symposium where a group of scientists examined the present crises in science and especially the "anti-science" movement.
DeBell, Garrett, *The Environmental Handbook* (New York: Ballantine Books, 1970).
  Indicates selected issues in the question of polution.
Huxley, Aldous, *Brave New World* (New York: Harper & Row, 1946).

A novel, now classic, which is set in the future and describes what the "future" might well be.

Lutz, Paul E. and Santmire, H. Paul, *Ecological Renewal* (Philadelphia: Fortress Press, 1972).

A stimulating paperback which describes the environmental crisis as seen by a biologist and by a theologian. Theological clues are discovered in the work of James Cone, Norman O. Brown, and Pierre Teilhard de Chardin.

Meadows, Donella H., *et al, The Limits to Growth:* A report for the Club of Rome's Project on the Predicament of Mankind (Washington: Potomac Books, 1972).

This celebrated book leads to a serious reconsideration of the generally accepted notion of "progress."

Thill, Georges, *La Fête Scientifique* (Paris: Desclée Brouwer, 1972).

A fascinating analysis of all the components, the social mechanisms, and the philosophical choices present in a well-defined scientific project.

EPILOGUE

The study of ethics is not a closed domain. We discussed the present crisis in morality, delineated viewpoints of human behavior and offered a vision of life based on the dialectics of justice and love. Action takes on meaning in the measure in which one truly accepts the significance of the other who is different from us, and in the measure in which one opens oneself to the task of really loving him. This love begins by accepting to be the object of a prior love which evokes a response.

The way in which this response can be expressed was investigated in various areas such as love, sexuality, marriage, authority, group living, economic and social life. Gradually, it appeared that we cannot limit ourselves to an individualistic point of view. There is much more involved than personal problems; it is a question involving everyone. This social dimension of our moral life cannot be reduced to the sum of particular cases, as is evident in the case of the sciences.

Finally, there remains a dimension of human existence which undoubtedly is dependent on a certain type of philosophical ethics, but which nevertheless is part of the human experience of those who reflect seriously on their lives. It is what Christians call the sense of the cross. Before the threat of failure, death or betrayal, there exists a possibility for man: to give himself up to his neighbor in a response of love with the admitted risk of seeing himself indeed fail, die or be betrayed. Such an attitude is considered by some as madness, by others as a scandal, by still others as supreme wisdom and as openness to life itself. It is not the task of an essay on ethics to decide these questions. It is for each man to face sooner or later; it is, without a doubt, the central problem for man today.